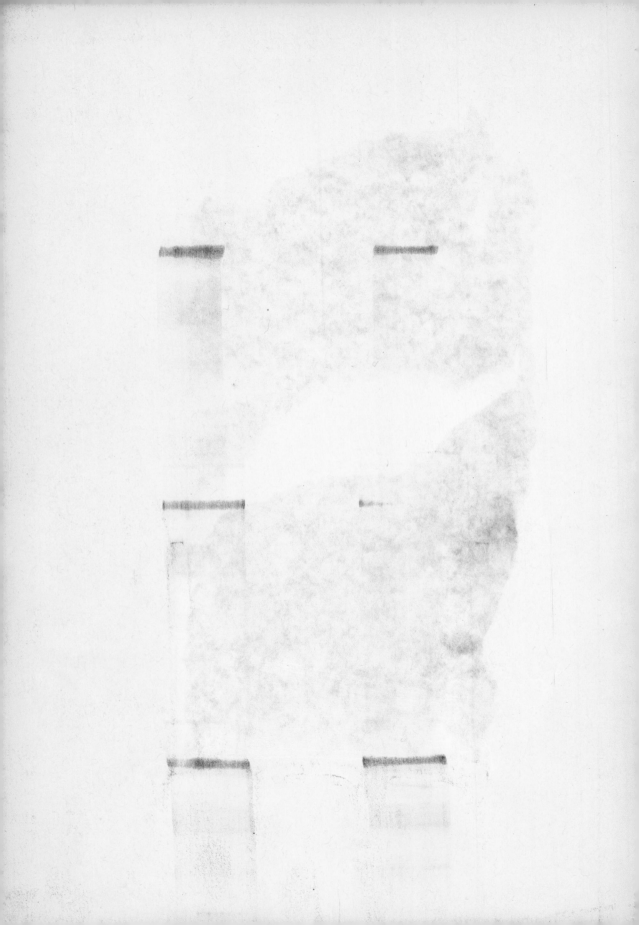

Front endpaper: "Raising the Liberty Pole, 1776." Title page: "Surrender of Lor

★ ★ ★ ★ ★ **HEROES OF THE**
American Revolution

*Could the American Revolution succeed? Through long and discouraging
years of war, it often seemed that the British would win. But there were
thousands of American patriots working and fighting for freedom.*

*This book presents dramatic closeups of eleven individual Americans who
struggled—on and off the battlefield—to make the Revolution succeed.*

Cornwallis at Yorktown'' (detail) by John Trumbull (Yale University Art Gallery).

★ ★ ★ HEROES OF THE

American Revolution

by Burke Davis

Illustrated with photographs, prints, and maps

RANDOM HOUSE NEW YORK

Trade Edition: ISBN: 0-394-82152-1   Library Edition: ISBN: 0-394-92152-6
Library of Congress Catalog Card Number: 79-136587
Manufactured in the United States of America

Designed by Murray M. Herman

Foreword ★ ★ ★ ★ ★ ★ ★

The leaders of the American Revolution may sometimes seem to us like supermen or saints or marble statues. But in truth they were all very human— men of weaknesses as well as strength, men of doubts as well as courage.

It is easy to understand why some patriots hesitated to sign the Declaration of Independence. If the rebels succeeded in establishing an independent nation, they would be heroes. But if the rebels lost, they would become outcasts and traitors. So the signers of the Declaration were risking their homes, their property, and probably their lives.

A successful revolution requires the talents of many kinds of people. The eleven men in this book have been chosen because they contributed to the American Revolution in a variety of ways. There are military and political leaders here, as well as an ambassador, a newspaper editor, and a spy. These accounts are intended for Americans growing up in a nation still stirred by radical ideas which had their birth two centuries ago.

BURKE DAVIS

★

CONTENTS

★

Paul Revere

Spy and Courier

In the soft spring dusk hundreds of British soldiers stood on Boston Common, waiting. Small boats were drawn up on shore, with oarsmen standing by. In full battle gear the troops of the British occupation force had been marched from their barracks and the Boston homes where they were quartered. Out in the Charles River, guarding the way to Charlestown on the mainland, lay the English warship *Somerset,* with her riding lights gleaming in the growing darkness. It was April 18, 1775. After a year of tension in the blockaded port city—then virtually an island—the redcoats were ready to strike.

The British were starting out for Concord, to seize firearms and ammunition stored there by rebellious American patriots. British General Thomas Gage had guarded his secret orders with great care. His spies and scouts had patrolled the road to Concord and Lexington, and tonight his officers lay in ambush, ready to seize any American courier who tried to carry a warning from Boston.

But now the secret was out. Young Lord Percy, the colonel of

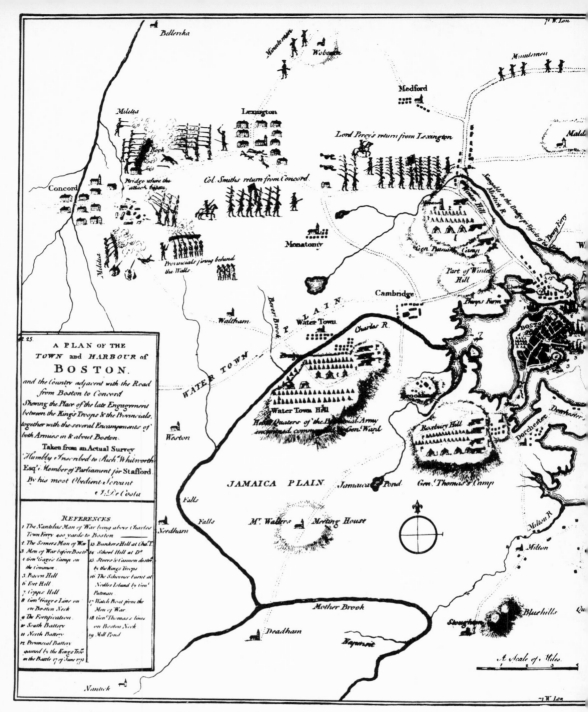

a British regiment, stood in the shadows of the Common, listening to the talk of American bystanders.

"The British have marched but they'll miss their aim."

"What aim?" Percy asked.

"Why, the cannon at Concord."

Salem
Halfway
Marblehead Rock

Lynn

Nahant Rock

Nahant Bay

Nahant Point

Hogg I.

BROAD

SOUND

Pudding
Point

Deer I.

North
Bruster

Nicker's Mate

Apthorps I.

Lovel I.

Little Brusters

Great Bruster

Egg I.

The prick'd line is the Ships Chanel

Rainforths I.

Point
Alderton

Hull

Hogg

Sheep I.

Porcupine I.

A British map drawn during the first days of the Revolution. The map shows Boston almost completely surrounded by water, with Concord and Lexington to the west.

Percy reported to General Gage. The rebels knew their plans —but the troops must march. The poorly organized Americans could not stop them. They probably would not fight.

Unknown to the British, an American spy network had learned of the march almost as soon as it was planned. The silversmith

Paul Revere had already ridden to Concord to warn other patriots to move guns and ammunition. And just the night before he had received three reports, all from men who heard British officers laughing and boasting: "There'll be hell to pay tomorrow." Revere and his friends made ready to warn rebel leaders on the mainland that the troops were coming. Lanterns would be hung in the steeple of Boston's Christ Church—one if the redcoats marched over the narrow Neck to the mainland, two if they went by water.

Tonight, as the British began to load into their boats on the Common, Paul Revere was busy. He hurried to the home of 23-year-old Robert Newman, the sexton of Christ Church, and told him to hang the lanterns. The silversmith then went to his own home to dress for the road. He would try to cross the river to carry the warning to the rebels of Concord tonight.

Near ten o'clock, when British boats began to cross, two lanterns glowed briefly in the church tower. Soon afterward Revere was ready for his journey. Two men waited at the waterside to row him across the river in a skiff. To deaden the sound of the oars one of the rebels wrapped them in a flannel petticoat donated by his sweetheart. The small boat pushed out into the dark water.

On the black hulk of the *Somerset* sentries were on watch, but Revere's boat crept soundlessly past. The night was chilly, a high tide was flooding in, and the moon was rising over the harbor. Still there was no hail from the *Somerset*. The skiff beached and Revere stepped ashore. He found a fine horse awaiting him, a slender, nervous mount from the stable of a wealthy Charlestown patriot. Like most New England horses, this one was small and wiry, bred for speed and endurance.

Revere left his friends at about 11 P.M. and rode down the moonlit road, slowly at first, since he feared an ambush. He knew that British officers were patrolling the roads in search of anyone carrying a message to the patriots. He trotted over a sandy neck toward the mainland between the Charles and Mystic rivers, his dark face alert, his body bent over the horse as he gained speed.

Revere was almost trapped at the start of his ride. Many years later he could recall every detail: "The moon shone bright. I had got almost over Charlestown Common towards Cambridge when I saw two Officers on Horseback, standing under the shade of a Tree, in the narrow part of the road. I was near enough to see their Holsters and Cockades."

One redcoat spurred his horse toward Revere, and the other turned up the Cambridge road to halt him if he should escape the first officer. Revere turned his horse and went at a full gallop into the Mystic road, gaining rapidly on his pursuer, who rode a heavy English horse. Within three hundred yards Revere looked back to see that he was drawing away. The redcoat's clumsy mount had stumbled into a shallow pond and was struggling in heavy clay. The British soldiers were soon left far behind. They had not fired a shot.

Revere clattered over a wooden bridge into Medford. "I awaked the Captain of the minute men," he said later, "and after that I alarmed almost every house till I got to Lexington." Behind him bells tolled, drums beat, and men shouted: "The regulars are out! Redcoats are coming!" Armed patriots—some of them sixteen or even younger—began to make their way toward Lexington. Revere flew ahead of the tumult, with a drumming of hooves along the deserted roads, halting at each darkened house to cry the alarm at the top of his voice.

Along another route toward the village rode a second courier, Revere's friend William Dawes. He too rode swiftly and well.

Revere recrossed the Mystic River and was on his way, through Menotomy and on into Lexington, bawling at every farmhouse, "The Regulars are out! Redcoats!"

The little horse flew on, now flecked with foam and heaving for breath. It was near midnight when Revere passed the green in Lexington. He rode to the home of the Reverend Jonas Clark, where John Hancock and John Adams and Mrs. Adams were sleeping, and where he found a guard of eight men surrounding the

At Lexington Green: The opening shots of the American Revolution.

house. Hancock and Adams were the two most important rebel leaders in New England, and the British had issued warrants for their arrest.

"Let me in," shouted Revere. "Message from Boston!"

"Quiet, man," the sergeant of the guard said. "The ladies and gentlemen told us not to disturb 'em with noise."

"Noise! They'll get noise enough. The Regulars are out!" He banged on the door. Clark's head appeared in an upper window.

"Call Mr. Hancock," Revere said.

Clark did not recognize the courier and ordered him away, but Hancock looked out. "Come in, Revere," he called. "We're not afraid of you."

The rider spent almost an hour in the house, telling the story of the British move, warning Hancock and Adams to flee. Hancock was indignant; he wanted to stay and fight. But Adams disagreed with him. Their place was in Philadelphia, he said, tending to the affairs of the Continental Congress.

About 1 A.M. Revere was off again, riding toward Concord with Billy Dawes and Samuel Prescott, a young doctor. They went rapidly along, arousing militiamen as they rode. Halfway between the towns, Revere was captured by British officers. His companions escaped. Paul described the scene later: "Out started six officers, seized my bridle, put their pistols to my breast, ordered me to dismount, which I did."

"Where are you from?" asked a redcoat.

"Boston," replied Revere.

"When did you leave there?"

"Eleven o'clock."

The officer whistled. "What's your name?"

"Revere."

"What! Paul Revere?"

"Yes."

The redcoats cursed him.

But Revere was defiant. "I've alarmed the country all the way up. We'll have five hundred men here soon."

The British led him away, one officer holding Revere's reins, and the others riding close-by. The redcoats threatened to kill him. But just before dawn, as sounds of the gathering militia grew louder, they set him free.

Revere, crossing Lexington Green in the misty sunrise, saw fifty or more armed farmers forming ranks. Church bells were ringing and women and children peered out from the houses.

Revere was in an upper room of a tavern, moving John Hancock's trunk, when he saw a British column approach. It was six companies strong, with bayonets gleaming in the early sunlight. Revere recognized Major Pitcairn of the Marines at the head of the column.

The silversmith hurried out with Hancock's trunk as the redcoats neared the Minutemen. Revere was some distance away when Captain John Parker of the militia called to his men, "Don't fire unless fired on. But if they mean to have a war let it begin here."

A shot rang out. The British charged forward and fired a volley.

Revere did not wait to see the outcome of the opening skirmish of the American Revolution, in which the redcoats killed eight militiamen. He rode back toward Cambridge. Behind him, the British moved on Concord, where they fired on the rebels and broke their ranks. But the redcoats were soon forced to fall back toward Boston under fire from militiamen and civilians who shot at them from farmhouses, fences, and woodlands. One of every nine of Pitcairn's redcoats was wounded or killed. The regulars lost their nerve and began to run.

The bloody struggle for American independence had opened. Within a few days the men of other colonies took up arms, ready to join the Massachusetts farmers.

It was not surprising that Paul Revere was in Lexington during the first combat of the Revolution. He had fought in the French and Indian War at the age of twenty-one. For fifteen years he had been a member of the Masonic Order, whose members were active in the growing rebellion against English rule. Revere joined not only the Sons of Liberty but also several other secret patriot clubs. He worked closely with Boston's leading radicals, John Hancock, Sam Adams, John Adams, Dr. Joseph Warren, and Dr. Benjamin Church.

Paul Revere grew up in the tumult of Boston's streets and wharves, served as a bell ringer at Christ Church, and studied for a time in Boston's North Grammar School. In his early teens he was apprenticed to a goldsmith. He mastered the smith's trade and soon he was learning other skills, including copperplate engraving and dentistry. Revere prospered and became a leader of Boston artisans and tradesmen. As clashes between British and Americans increased, the radical leaders of Boston depended upon Revere to enlist these workmen for the patriot cause. And when Boston patriots staged a parade or a protest, the men in the streets were most often the men organized by Paul Revere.

Paul first married Sarah Orne, who bore him eight children. After her death he married Rachel Walker, who bore him eight more. Revere turned out beautiful silverware, and became one of New England's most popular craftsmen. His pieces are still treasured two centuries later.

In the ten years before the Revolution, Revere made many copper engravings, cartoons, advertising cards, and portraits. Though most of his work was copied from others, his political cartoons attacking British colonial policies were very popular. Through his cartoons he became a leading patriot propagandist, aiding the cause of revolution.

After the so-called "Boston Massacre" in 1770, when British soldiers killed a few members of an unruly mob, Revere made the most famous of his engravings. Copied from a drawing by a Boston artist named Henry Pelham, it is a rather crude engraving of red-

Paul Revere's version of the Boston Massacre.

coats massacring innocent civilians in cold blood. This print sold rapidly and became effective patriot propaganda. For the next few years Revere made other engravings on the anniversary of the massacre to help keep alive the resentment of Bostonians.

As the Revolution drew near, the silversmith became more deeply involved in the rebel cause. In December 1773 he took a leading part in the Boston Tea Party. Revere joined a group of patriots who daubed their faces with soot and red paint and tied a few feathers in their hair to masquerade as "Mohawks." The silversmith helped to dump cargoes of tea into Boston harbor in protest against new British taxes.

The tea thrown overboard by the Bostonians soon marked the high tide on beaches many miles away. The drifting tea helped to unite the thirteen American colonies. As one patriot leader said in distant Williamsburg, "The tea that was cast into the sea in Massachusetts will soon wash ashore in Virginia."

More than £18,000 worth of cargo had been ruined, but the "Mohawks" had not run wild as other mobs of Bostonians had done in recent months. The Boston Tea Party had been carefully planned to challenge British policies.

No one doubted that Parliament's revenge would be swift and severe.

Most of the "Mohawks" went home, but there was no rest for Paul Revere. Express riders were needed to carry news of the Tea Party to other cities. The silversmith, as one of the most experienced of Boston's rebel couriers, left to carry the news to Pennsylvania leaders in Philadelphia. Riding a sturdy pony, he galloped through Cambridge, Watertown, Worcester and Springfield, Hartford, New Haven, and into New York, halting only to change horses and call out the news. He kept up a strenuous pace to Philadelphia, riding an average of sixty-three miles a day, over roads deep in mud, ice, and snow. To the surprise of friends he was back in Boston just eleven days after his departure. He brought cheering news from the south: patriots of other colonies would stand by Massachusetts, and no Atlantic port would accept British tea.

In May, as soon as orders could cross the Atlantic, London punished the rebellious city. Boston's port was closed to all shipping. Trade came to a halt. Thousands of Bostonians were thrown out of work and their families went hungry. General Gage arrived as the new governor, bringing eleven regiments of redcoats. Citizens were forbidden to hold town meetings. The British were determined to choke Massachusetts into obedience.

Protest meetings were held in other colonies, and food supplies

were sent overland for the relief of Boston. The harsh punishment of Massachusetts helped to unify the colonies. In Virginia, George Washington, a man slow to wrath, was so outraged that he began to speak of war against England.

Boston's rebels met outside the city and drew up a manifesto known as the Suffolk Resolves. Revere carried the radical document to the first Continental Congress, meeting in Philadelphia. The Congress itself was a sign that Americans were aroused, for the thirteen colonies had bickered among themselves for almost a

The Boston Tea Party. The "Mohawks" included 13-year-old Peter Slater and 15-year-old Joshua Wyeth.

Paul Revere, silversmith, as portrayed by John Singleton Copley. (Copley, a Boston Tory, moved to England during the Revolution.)

century, unable to agree on the simplest of their problems.

The Suffolk Resolves sounded much like a declaration of war upon Great Britain, and some timid Congressmen from the South feared them. But Congress approved the New England manifesto, and Revere hurried home with the news. He found that Boston had become an armed camp. The British were fortifying the city. New England militia, some of whom were called Minutemen, were drilling in nearby towns.

Revere became the leader of patriot spies in Boston, keeping close watch on the redcoats. As the year 1775 opened, an armed clash seemed inevitable. Less than four months later Paul Revere was to make his ride to Lexington on the day the war began.

After the battles of Lexington and Concord, Revere became an artillery officer and served on an ill-fated American expedition into Maine. His time in uniform was short, for the new nation soon found other uses for his talents. He cast cannon and made gunpowder. He also engraved and printed the paper currency of Massachusetts, making some plates for banknotes on the reverse of his Boston Massacre plate.

When the war was over Revere continued his work as a silver-smith, but found other interests as well. He cast hundreds of church bells, many of them still in use throughout New England. He cast cannon for the U.S. Army. In 1795 he did all the brass and copper work for the *Constitution*, the first important U.S. warship, which became known as "Old Ironsides" and is still in existence. In 1800 Revere founded the first mill in America for rolling sheet copper, the Revere Copper and Brass Company, which still bears his name.

Revere died in 1818 at the age of eighty-three, honored for his long and useful life as a businessman and patriot. Henry Wadsworth Longfellow had not yet written his poem about the midnight ride and few people of the time remembered that dramatic incident of so long before. But Paul Revere has come down in American affections as the brave courier of the Revolution. Two centuries later his name raises echoes of galloping hooves along country roads, a voice in the blackness calling an alarm, a rap on the door, and a fading cry, "The redcoats are coming!"

John Adams

Mastermind of Rebellion

In the first hot days of June 1775, Philadelphia's crowded State House was loud with talk of war. Speaker after speaker rose to face the anxious representatives of the thirteen colonies. Some shouted threats to England, the world's greatest military power. Softer voices urged caution and new efforts for peace.

The defiant speakers were chiefly New Englanders, to whom war had already come. It was now two months since the fighting at Lexington and Concord, and the redcoat army was penned inside Boston by a rabble of New England volunteers. The Second Continental Congress was trying desperately to plan for an uncertain future, dreading a final break with England. If these men declared independence, and then failed to win their revolution, they would be hanged as traitors. For many centuries no nation had successfully broken away from a monarch to establish self-government.

Like Americans as a whole, Congress was deeply divided. To those who hesitated, and to those who were loyal to Great Britain, the New Englanders spoke of the growing danger from a large British army in America. These men from the north tried hard to arouse others to the threat of more bloodshed. In Philadelphia the feeling of tension grew daily. Except for Congress, there was no American government. There was no army or navy.

On June 14 John Adams, a lawyer from Massachusetts, knew that the time had come for action. Before the day's session opened he walked in the State House yard with his cousin Sam Adams, talking of what must be done. Congress should adopt the volunteer army outside Boston as its own—but first the Southern aristocrats in Congress must be won over. John Adams was ready to propose as Commander in Chief a Southerner—George Washington of Virginia. He was the one man all the groups within Congress might accept.

The men who went into the State House hall that morning wore the fashionable wigs and knee pants of the day, for they were civilians—all but one. In a corner of the room sat a tall, pale man in the blue and scarlet uniform of a colonel of Virginia militia. He was George Washington, a delegate who did not join the debate that day. He seldom made speeches.

Delegates looked up in surprise as John Adams began his brief speech. He moved that Congress adopt the army at Cambridge and send it a commanding general. Adams saw displeasure on several faces but hurried on. He had carefully considered every American leader and was ready to nominate one as Commander in Chief. "I declare without hesitation that there is but one gentleman in my mind for this important command."

John Hancock of Massachusetts, who was presiding, looked about with an expectant smile. He was a close friend of Adams. Although Hancock had never been a soldier, he fancied himself as a leader of vast armies.

"The gentleman I have in mind," continued John Adams, "is from Virginia. . . ."

Washington left his seat and darted into the adjoining library, as if embarrassed to hear himself praised.

Hancock's smile was gone. Adams later wrote, "I never saw a more sudden and sinking Change of Countenance."

Hancock stared sullenly ahead as Adams spoke. The disappointed leader from Massachusetts did not realize that Adams was supporting Washington in order to draw the rich Southern colonies into the struggle. Gradually it was becoming clear that John Adams, perhaps more than any other rebel leader, was trying to make America into a nation, and not merely a collection of colonies. His great contribution to the Revolution was his insistence upon a union. To accomplish this he had talked privately with almost all the Congressmen, overcoming opposition.

The modest Colonel Washington did not return to the room that day or the next. There was some opposition to the Virginian but John argued that though Washington had little experience as a commander, he was the best man to be had. The other delegates were won over in private talks. John made a brief, modest report of this in his diary: "Pains were taken out of doors to obtain an unanimity." Washington learned of his selection only when some members left the State House at dinner time on June 15, shook his hand, and addressed him as "General."

Adams was pleased with his success. He wrote his wife Abigail that "the modest, virtuous, amiable, generous and brave George Washington" was now in command, and would help unify the country. Adams was pleasantly surprised when Washington made a brief speech of acceptance—and refused to take a penny in salary, however long the war might last. (The general did turn in a large expense account at the end of the war.) Adams marveled that this wealthy man would leave a pleasant life on his large plantation to lead such a dangerous and unpromising rebellion, knowing that if he failed he would lose his beloved Mount Vernon—and probably his life as well.

John Adams, a drawing made just after he left the Presidency.

Adams had spent years in guiding first Massachusetts and then other colonies toward a break with England, always working behind the scenes, plotting the moves of resistance to be made by others. Now, as he saw Washington and a few officers leave Philadelphia on June 23, on their way to join the army outside Boston, Congressman Adams was envious. He admired the band music and the smartly dressed troops of Washington's escort. That day he wrote in his diary, "Such is the pride and pomp of war. I, poor creature, worn out with scribbling for my bread and my liberty, low in spirits and weak in health, must leave others to wear the laurels which I have sown; others to eat the bread which I have earned."

This was not a passing mood, but though Adams longed to meet the British in battle, he was never to wear a uniform. His role was to be that of a "father" to the Revolution, guiding public sentiment and forcing other rebel leaders so far toward an open break with England that there could be no retreat.

John Adams did not look the part of a rebel plotter. He was a plump little man of forty years, though he seemed much younger, with his soft, almost girlish face and his Cupid's bow mouth. But Adams was proud and highly intelligent and above all completely, painfully honest. He was the only leading American rebel who kept a full and revealing diary, and into its pages he poured all of his thoughts.

He did not lead the way to revolution lightly, for he revered the heritage of English freedom, and "our British ancestors, who have defended for us the inherent rights of mankind, against kings and cruel priests, in short against the gates of earth and hell." When he saw that his course must lead to war with England he wrote, "I go mourning in my Heart all the Day long." And yet, on the day George Washington left Philadelphia and the final step toward war had been taken, the alert Adams looked far ahead. He carefully planned how to turn the rebellion toward future victory. He placed an informer, his own secretary, William Tudor, on

Washington's staff. Adams ordered Tudor to report on every detail of army life, "for I am determined that I will know that army and the character of all its officers." John Adams left nothing to chance.

John Adams was born just outside Boston, in Braintree, Massachusetts, in 1734. His father was a local official and militia officer who directed most of the town's affairs for twenty years. The family always took a leading part in town meetings, an early example of American democracy at work. John's parents encouraged his natural independence of spirit, and taught him that he must answer only to his conscience.

John went to Harvard College, where he was a brilliant scholar. After teaching school briefly at Worcester, Massachusetts, he took up the practice of law and moved to Boston. There he became a friend of James Otis, a well-known New England lawyer of the time. Otis was a gifted orator who often protested that the British were denying Americans their rights. When Parliament passed a new tax law called the Stamp Act, ten years before the Revolution, Otis so aroused Bostonians that mobs ran wild in the city.

John Adams opposed such violence as firmly as he opposed the Stamp Act itself. But in a newspaper article he echoed the cry of Otis, "No taxation without representation!" Adams argued that Americans had God-given rights as free men, and that citizens of all the colonies should resist attacks upon their liberties. "If ever an infant country deserved to be cherished," he wrote, "it is America." The article was so effective that John became the penman of the rebel cause in New England.

John was delighted when patriots in the colonies drove the distributors of the new stamps from office, even though this meant the closing of customs houses and courts. He and the firebrand Sam Adams whipped public feelings in Boston to a fever pitch. The cousins seemed to have only their devotion to the revolutionary cause in common. Sam, though he looked to be a quiet, mild,

Bostonians gleefully burning the hated tax stamps.

and rather delicate young man, was a fanatic, fearless and reckless.

Between them the Adams cousins enlisted most of the leading rebels in Massachusetts. Many years before the outbreak of war they carefully studied their friends, choosing some as future patriot leaders who would stand firm in a crisis. Boston became the capital of rebellion many years before war finally came, and the Adams

influence was chiefly responsible for the endless agitation in the
city. John and Sam led the way, urging patriots of other colonies
to follow.

Sam Adams persuaded their wealthy young friend John Hancock to join them. John helped to attract others, including Paul
Revere, Dr. Joseph Warren, and Dr. Benjamin Church (who was
later found to be a spy for the British). The Adams cousins helped
to form the new radical group, the Sons of Liberty, who met se-
cretly to plot against the British. Under Sam's leadership the rebel
movement grew steadily more daring. Patriot mobs often raced
through the city streets in disguise, armed with clubs, frightening
government officials and sacking their homes. John feared that
such violence would lead to bloodshed. His fears were realized in
the winter of 1770 when British soldiers killed five civilians in the
"Boston Massacre."

New Englanders demanded revenge. But John Adams thought
the redcoats deserved a fair trial. When other lawyers refused to
accept these unpopular clients, he joined his friend Josiah Quincy
in their defense. Adams and Quincy won acquittal on the grounds
of self-defense for the British commander, Captain John Preston,
and for six of the eight soldiers on trial. Two others, found guilty
of manslaughter, were branded on their thumbs with a hot iron.

Sam Adams and other patriots criticized John, saying that a ver-
dict of guilty against the redcoats would help to arouse the colonists against England. But John clung to his convictions. The law,
he said, must be respected and obeyed, whatever the excitements
and public mood of the time. In a free country, all men must have
the right to defense against their accusers.

Others approved. John was elected to represent Boston in the
General Court, the legislature of Massachusetts. But he did not
hold his seat for long. Royal Governor Thomas Hutchinson, who
had the power to veto representatives elected by the voters, rejected John "for the very conspicuous part Mr. Adams has played
in opposition."

In 1773, when a new British tax provoked the Boston Tea Party, John did not take part. But in this case he applauded the work of the mob: "This is the most magnificent move of all! There is a dignity, a majesty . . . in this last effort of the patriots that I greatly admire. The people should never rise without doing something to be remembered—something notable and striking. This destruction of the tea is so bold, so daring, so firm, intrepid and inflexible, and it must have so important consequences . . . that I consider it as an epoch in history."

When the British responded by closing Boston's port, and war became inevitable, John and Sam Adams were elected to the first Continental Congress from Massachusetts. In the spring of 1775 the cousins again went to Philadelphia, where the delegates from all thirteen colonies met beyond the reach of English troops. John worked there to unify the colonies and organize the country for a long war.

After George Washington rode off to Boston, Adams fought even harder to lead Congress to declare independence—and to create a single nation from the thirteen quarrelsome colonies. After months of effort he wrote of the effects of "this incessant round of thinking and speaking upon the greatest subjects that ever employed the mind of man. . . . I am wearied to death; some of you younger folk must take your trick, and let me sleep." Few Congressmen were interested and some were openly hostile, but John Adams gave them no peace. During the long session of 1776 he was forever writing, speaking, persuading, or plotting to create a separate nation. Adams confided to his wife, "This country knows not, and never can know, the torments I have endured for its sake."

He drove Congress to action largely by his earnest speeches and force of logic. When Congress sought independence at last, young Thomas Jefferson was named chairman of a committee to draft a declaration, with Adams as one of the members. Adams persuaded Jefferson to write the document, suggested a couple of small

New England rebels tarred-and-feathered a few tax officials. This English cartoon included the Boston Tea Party in the background.

changes in his draft, and helped win the approval of Congress.

Adams urged the states to set up governments of their own—the first systems of modern democratic self-government. He wrote a plan for governing Massachusetts and drew up its constitution. He planned much of the organization of the American army. And he insisted that General Washington must have full authority, subject only to the control of Congress.

The most important of his work was done, but Adams helped in many other ways to launch the new American nation. As Chairman of the Board of War, he was what we would call Secretary of Defense. Adams opposed members from the smaller states when they insisted upon states' rights, because he thought the central government should be supreme. "The confederacy is to make us one individual only," he said. "It is to form us, like separate parcels of metal, into one common mass. We shall no longer retain our separate individuality, but become a single individual."

After more than two years of war Adams went to Paris as an American Commissioner, where he aided Benjamin Franklin in important negotiations with the French. He returned home to join the struggle to draft and adopt the Constitution. And when George Washington became the first U.S. President, John Adams was named Vice President. Eight years later he was elected second President of the United States.

It was only in 1801, at the age of sixty-six, that Adams realized his old dream of returning to his farm at Braintree (which was now called Quincy).

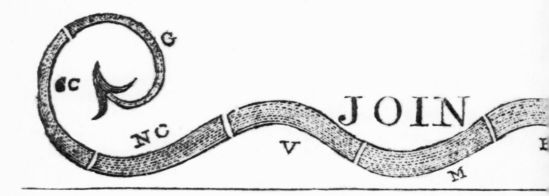

John lived to see his son, John Quincy Adams, become sixth President of the United States. But at last, on July 4, 1826, the fiftieth anniversary of the Declaration of Independence, John Adams died at the age of ninety. His last thoughts were of another surviving hero of the revolution. The old man roused himself and spoke with great effort: "Thomas Jefferson survives." Soon afterward he was gone. He did not know that Jefferson had died just a few hours earlier on the same day.

The country mourned Adams as one of the true founders of the United States, for many remembered the boldness of his leadership in the days when rebellion had been dangerous indeed. As Congressman Richard Stockton of New Jersey had written long before, in the days of the nation's birth, "The man to whom the country is most indebted . . . is Mr. John Adams of Boston." The little lawyer from Braintree was remembered as the giant of the Revolution.

John Adams worked constantly to unify the thirteen colonies. His ideas were well expressed in this patriotic drawing by Paul Revere, based on an earlier cartoon published by Benjamin Franklin.

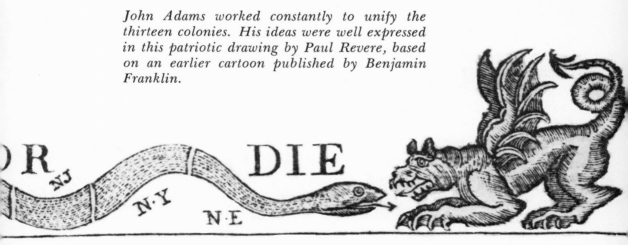

Henry Knox

Self-Taught Master of Artillery

As the spring of 1775 passed into summer, the long line of trenches grew about Boston. Thousands of New England boys who had joined the new army to fight the British found themselves digging instead, toiling with pick and shovel in the hard soil day after day. Most of the troops were farm boys, accustomed to hard labor, but they had never known such exhausting work as this. Officers told them that they were keeping the redcoats cooped inside the city, and that the enemy would soon be driven away.

The line of fortifications crept along the hills surrounding Boston harbor, from the Mystic River on the north, past Cambridge and the Charles River, through the outlying village of Roxbury, and to Dorchester Heights on the south, at the edge of the sea.

In Roxbury, where small forts were rising, the officer in charge of the volunteers was Henry Knox, a 25-year-old Boston bookseller who weighed almost three hundred pounds. This enormous, jolly artilleryman had learned what he knew of cannon and fortifications from books in his shop. In this unofficial army, he was called

"Colonel" by his men. But in truth he was only a civilian, since Congress had not approved his rank.

Still, the men worked as he directed, for he had the air of a man who knew what he was about and a charming way of persuading others to follow his orders. He was also one of the army's grand sights, always in a well-tailored uniform and gleaming boots, amid the swarm of dirty, tattered soldiers. Soon the strongest forts in the line were those of bookseller Knox.

In July 1775, when the salt marshes before Boston steamed under the sun and heat waves shimmered over the occupied city, George Washington arrived in Cambridge to take command. He had been nine days on the road from Philadelphia. Now the informal New England army became the Continental Army.

From the hills of the mainland the new Commander in Chief stared down through his glass at besieged Boston and at the British warships in the harbor. For days Washington rode the ten miles of trenches and small forts encircling the city, puzzling over how he might force the British from the city. One who usually rode with him was Henry Knox. The commander liked the way the laughing young man talked of the siege. He also admired the learning of Knox, his easy manners, and the smart uniforms he wore.

At first the siege seemed simple. Boston was surrounded by a large army of New Englanders. Since its only link to the mainland was a narrow causeway (as shown on the map on page 4), the British garrison appeared to be helpless.

But as weeks passed, thousands of the New England farm boys returned home. Washington's officers squabbled. In vain he begged Congress for supplies and ammunition. The redcoats were there in full view of his telescope, waiting, hoping to stamp out the American rebellion at its start. Washington could do little more than watch the enemy. He spent most of his time merely holding his army together. Gloom settled about his headquarters in Cambridge.

The British had hundreds of cannon in position in Boston, to say nothing of the guns of the British fleet. Until he had heavy cannon Washington could not attack the enemy. When he saw that he must have an artillery corps of his own, he chose Henry Knox as its commander. It was one of the most fortunate American appointments of the war. Knox was delighted with his new post, but he knew that there was no American artillery to command. He suggested that captured British cannon be brought from Fort Ticonderoga.

Washington agreed. He ordered Knox to haul to Cambridge the big guns that had been captured from the British by Ethan Allen and his Green Mountain Boys, a raiding band of militia from Vermont. Allen's daring blow, the first real American offensive of the war, had blocked the important military road from Canada.

The task seemed impossible. But Knox left at once, as cheerfully as if he were opening his bookshop for the day. The army had no money, and Henry had to pay teamsters and hire oxen himself. Fort Ticonderoga was in distant northern New York State, between Lake Champlain and Lake George. The guns must be dragged over more than three hundred miles of rough roads, several river crossings, and the rocky slopes of the Berkshire Hills —all in mid-winter.

At Ticonderoga, Knox found that most of the cannon were old and useless. But he chose about sixty of the best ones and ordered them loaded on boats to float down Lake George. The sixty guns together weighed 120,000 pounds. Knox also carried more than a ton of lead and a barrel of musket flints, since the best such stone in America was found near Ticonderoga. Scores of men with ropes and pulleys wrestled with the heavy loads.

The flotilla set off on December 9 in a flat-bottomed scow and two smaller sailing vessels, the overloaded boats beating southward through icy waters, the crews often forced to row into the teeth of strong winds. The scow struck a rock and sank with the largest of the guns. The men raised them and repaired the scow. Then they

The long trek: Henry Knox's men drag British cannon from Ticonderoga to Boston (by a twentieth-century artist).

had to rest for a day, huddling beside a fire in weather so bitter that they almost froze. Knox then urged them onward until they reached Fort George at the south end of the lake, where he had assembled horses, 160 oxen, and sleds for the long overland journey.

Knox wrote to patriot leaders along his route, asking for food and shelter and spare teams. He also ordered big mortar shells shipped from New York to Cambridge so that he could open fire on the enemy when his long journey was over.

After a maddening delay at Fort George, during which he haggled with greedy contractors over the hire of oxen, Knox reached a bargain. The procession moved on once more. The huge Knox sometimes led the way on horseback, but often he rode back and forth to see that all was moving as planned. The party passed Glens Falls, where civilians stared curiously at them, and dined in Saratoga on Christmas Eve. The next day, after fighting their way through a two-foot snowfall, they reached New City, nine miles above Albany, New York.

Horses gave out and were left behind. Knox and his men stumbled ahead on foot, reaching Albany "almost perished with the cold." One of the big guns fell into the Hudson River and had to be recovered. And still another fell into deep water as the caravan crossed the frozen river near Albany. Citizens of the city were so enthusiastic that they paid the hired teamsters to allow them to help drag the guns across the river.

Knox and his men now moved along the old Post Road east of the Hudson. Reaching the western border of Massachusetts, they entered the Berkshire Hills and turned eastward over what is now Route 23, in those days a treacherous track leading through a dense evergreen forest. They crossed a mountain pass where there is today no road. They struggled up and down rocky hills, skirting deep chasms below. In the lowlands they had to cross half-frozen swamps. They eased their giant guns down the eastern slopes of the Berkshires by using drag chains and poles thrust under sled runners, and ropes tied to trees, to prevent sleds from crushing animals and men before them.

In Springfield, with snow disappearing rapidly, Knox lost his New York teamsters, who returned to their homes. Now Massachusetts teamsters took over for the last leg of the trip. The ground froze again a few nights later, and the sleds were more easily dragged to Framingham by oxen, and thence into Cambridge. The incredible journey ended at last, after forty days of struggle. Washington could now threaten to bombard Boston to drive out the British garrison. With the guns of Fort Ticonderoga, Washington fortified the hills overlooking the city. Henry Knox had created the first American artillery corps.

One night in March 1776, under cover of fire from a few of these cannon, American troops hauled artillery up Dorchester Heights and built an imposing row of breastworks. At dawn the British looked up to see that they were completely ringed by big guns, and that the city could no longer be held. A few days later the redcoats left Boston and the jubilant American troops entered the city.

For years afterward, gunners laughed over the story of their colonel's return to Boston. As Knox rode past the Reverend Mather Byles, a noted punster who was a Tory sympathizer, the preacher pointed to the huge figure riding at Washington's side and cried, "I never saw a (Kn)ox fatter in my life."

The first great victory of the war had been made possible by Knox and his long-suffering teamsters. But the army could not repay the colonel the heavy costs of dragging in the guns from Ticonderoga, and it was to be many years before he collected the $2,500 due him.

Henry Knox was one of ten sons of a shipmaster who lost his money and abandoned his family, forcing the 9-year-old Henry to leave school and work to help support his mother and the younger children. The boy found a place in a Boston bookstore, where he educated himself by reading most of the books on the shelves. He studied Plutarch's *Lives* until he knew the legends of ancient heroes by heart. He read books in French to master the language. And as he grew older Henry read and reread books on military history and engineering.

In his teens Henry became famous as a strongman among the youth of Boston. He was a towering figure with muscular arms and huge fists, a leader of a South Boston gang which often staged street fights with rivals. Knox and his young comrades joined an artillery company organized by British soldiers. This company, known as "The Train," became celebrated in Boston for its smart appearance, rigid discipline, and the handling of its three brass guns.

Knox worked hard at the bookstore. As soon as he became twenty-one and could legally do so, he opened his own New London Book Store. He stocked it with books imported from England, textbooks, Bibles, London magazines, and stationery. Knox also published new books. He advertised a cure for the bites of mad dogs, as well as wallpaper, musical and scientific instruments, and snuff. His shop became an intellectual center of Boston. As its host young Henry was noted for his gracious manners, for his broad education gained from reading, and for his dapper dress. In 1774 he married Lucy Flucker, the daughter of the Royal Secretary of the Province, despite objections by her parents.

Knox refused a commission in the British army offered by his father-in-law. Instead, he drilled his artillerymen of "The Train" and studied military tactics more industriously than ever. He was by now a lieutenant of his gunnery unit, skilled at firing the big weapons despite the loss of two fingers in a hunting accident. Henry also made friends of leading New England patriots who came to his shop. One was the Boston silversmith and engraver, Paul Revere. Another was a young Rhode Island manufacturer, Nathanael Greene.

Knox first saw bloodshed in December 1770, when he witnessed

the "Boston Massacre." The 20-year-old bookseller tried in vain
to prevent the British from firing on the unarmed civilian mob
that was taunting the troops.

In the spring of 1775, when war was in the air and a patriot
army was gathering outside Boston, Knox and his wife slipped
through the lines one night, eluding redcoat sentries. He joined
the army in Cambridge, was put to work building forts, and was
there when George Washington arrived to take command.

After Knox's cannon made possible the rebel victory at Boston,
the war moved away from New England into other regions. A
British invasion force of 32,000 men landed on Staten Island near
New York. And despite the guns Henry Knox placed nearby,
enemy warships moved freely in the waters about New York. His
short-range cannon often burst, causing more American than British casualties, and their shells could not reach the enemy ships. In
disastrous defeats on Long Island, in lower Manhattan, and in
White Plains, American artillerymen fought gallantly but were
overwhelmed. Knox and several officers narrowly escaped capture
in New York and their guns were abandoned. The army was de-

*An American cannon in the Revolution, sketched by the artist Charles
Willson Peale. The screw was used to raise and lower the barrel.
(Peale served as an officer in Washington's army at Trenton and
Princeton.)*

The Battle of Princeton, by James Peale. Like his father, Charles Willson Peale, the artist was serving under General Washington at the time.

feated again at Harlem Heights, where Knox arrived exhausted, complaining, "I have not had my clothes off anights for more than forty days."

Like Washington, Knox was dismayed by the cowardice of some American troops, who had run from British bayonets. But both realized that these men needed only leadership and training to become good soldiers. Knox looked into the future. "We must have a standing army," he wrote. "The militia get sick, or think themselves so; they spread a panic." He recommended that "we ought to have academies in which the whole theory of the art of war shall be taught." The 26-year-old officer with one year's military service sent to Congressman John Adams a complete plan for a military academy. Because of the far-sighted plans he drew in the days of disastrous defeats around New York, Henry Knox can properly be called the father of the U.S. Military Academy at West Point.

The rebel army retreated into New Jersey—by now, as Knox said, "only a receptacle for ragamuffins." Washington's force had dwindled from 20,000 to 4000 men, 585 of them in the artillery. But the small corps of gunners was learning its trade.

After months of defeat, Washington and his officers planned a bold stroke against the enemy at Trenton—unexpected because it was launched in midwinter. When the little American army crossed the icy Delaware River on Christmas night of 1776, Knox supervised the loading of the boats and the handling of the eighteen cannon. His gun crews cleared all the streets of Trenton and made the surprise victory possible. One of Knox's sergeants wrote of the climax of the battle, "We loaded with canister shot, and let them come nearer. We fired altogether again and such destruction it made, you cannot conceive—the bridge looked red as blood, with their killed and wounded and their red coats. The enemy beat a retreat." The British forces could hardly believe that the tattered Americans handled guns so well.

After Trenton, Knox was praised highly in Washington's reports to Congress. By now, promoted to general of artillery, Knox was always in Washington's councils and beside him in battle. He became known as one of the army's most talented and reliable officers. Henry wrote his wife, "People are more lavish in their praises of my poor endeavors than they deserve. All the merit I can claim is my industry. . . . The attack of Trenton was a most horrid scene. War, my Lucy, is not a humane trade."

The artillery saved the army again a few days later, at the battle of Princeton. The army settled in a miserable winter camp at Morristown, New Jersey. Knox spent weeks in Boston, ordering new cannon, enlisting volunteers for the army, and planning construction of the first U.S. arsenal to build and store weapons.

In camp at Valley Forge the following winter, the artillery was organized for the first time into four battalions. By 1778, Knox had forty-four companies in his four regiments, and his gunners had become a professional corps. Despite poor equipment, they fought well in every engagement of the Revolution.

After the war Henry Knox succeeded George Washington in command of the army. Later, as a member of President Washington's Cabinet, Knox was the first U.S. Secretary of War.

He settled in Maine, where he acquired thirty square miles of land, much of which he sold to meet his debts. Though he had lived through many battles and other perils, the general met death in a simple household accident. In 1806, at the age of fifty-six, he died after swallowing a chicken bone.

He left his family the handsome mansion, Montpelier, in Thomaston. He also left behind a military tradition that had been admired by a French volunteer officer, the Marquis de Lafayette, many years before: "You fire better than the French! Upon my honor, I speak the truth! The progress of your artillery is regarded by everybody as one of the wonders of the Revolution."

Thomas Jefferson: A bust made by the French sculptor Jean Houdon, when Jefferson was in France after the Revolution.

Thomas Jefferson

Declarer of Independence

On May 14, 1776, a 33-year-old Virginian rode into Philadelphia to take his seat in a Congress seething with excitement. The movement toward American independence was nearing its climax. The newcomer, Thomas Jefferson, though he was one of the youngest Congressmen, was welcomed as a leader of the bold plan to create a new nation.

Jefferson was an imposing figure, strikingly erect, almost six feet three inches tall, spare and rawboned. As the overseer of his Virginia plantation said, he was "like a fine horse, he had no surplus flesh." His hands and feet were large. His face was long, square-jawed, and freckled, with a high, pointed nose. There was an expression of intelligence and good humor on his face; he seemed to take notice of everything. He had an odd habit of humming to himself in moments of silence.

Jefferson arrived with saddlebags bulging with money he had collected. He intended to buy gunpowder for Virginia troops. And he wanted to send supplies for the relief of the unfortunate people of Boston whose port had been occupied by the British.

Although Americans had been at war against the British for more than a year, the colonies had not yet "separated" from Great Britain. Before he left home Jefferson had read a fiery new pamphlet called *Common Sense* by Thomas Paine, an appeal for a new democratic government for Americans. Jefferson had been writing in the same vein during recent months, urging Virginians toward independence.

In Philadelphia, Jefferson found waiting for him a letter from

Jefferson used this machine, a polygraph, to copy automatically what he was writing.

John Page, a boyhood friend from Virginia. "For God's sake," wrote Page, "declare the Colonies independent at once and save us from ruin." Such pleas were pouring into Philadelphia from all thirteen colonies.

Jefferson settled in two rented rooms in a house at the corner of Market and 7th Streets, in the three-story brick home of Jacob Graff, a young bricklayer. The Virginian had a bedroom and parlor on the second floor separated by the stairway. Jefferson probably followed the routine he had known since boyhood—up at 6 A.M. for exercise, washing his feet in cold water to ward off colds, then breakfast and the day's work.

Because of his reputation as a forceful writer, Jefferson was put to work at once by Congress as well as by his fellow Virginians. He worked almost endlessly, writing committee reports and many other documents, among them a new constitution for Virginia. He wrote on a folding writing box of his own design which was made for him by a Philadelphia craftsman.

Back in Virginia, Jefferson's friends of the Revolutionary Convention, meeting in the Capitol at Williamsburg, took a bold step toward establishing a new nation. Soon after the flight of the royal governor, they instructed their delegates in Congress to declare for independence. This resolution was hurried to Philadelphia. On June 7 Jefferson's colleague in Congress, Richard Henry Lee, presented the Virginia resolution:

> Resolved, That these United Colonies, are and of right ought to be, free and independent States, that they are absolved from all allegiance to the British Crown, and that all political connection between them and the State of Great Britain is, and ought to be, totally dissolved.

This was the fateful step toward which Congress had been moving for almost two years but which it had not yet dared to take. Virginia's resolution set off a bitter debate. Richard Henry Lee and George Wythe of Virginia and John Adams of Massachusetts led the fight for the resolution. But they met stout resistance from conservatives who called themselves "the sensible part of the House." The opponents were led by James Wilson and John Dickinson of Pennsylvania and Edward Rutledge of South Carolina. The conservatives said they wanted eventual independence, but that the time was not yet ripe. They believed their goals could be won without war and violence. Dickinson said, "The cause of liberty is a cause of too much dignity to be sullied by turbulence and tumult."

Lee, Wythe, and Adams argued that Americans were waiting for Congress to lead the way and that only after independence had been declared would European nations be willing to form alliances and provide troops and supplies.

Congress was dangerously divided. Colonies most threatened by British troops and warships favored immediate independence. Others were reluctant. The delegations from New Jersey, Maryland, and Delaware joined Pennsylvania, New York, and South Carolina in opposing immediate independence. Georgia and all of New England supported the Virginians. On June 10 leaders suspended discussion, fearing that it would tear Congress apart.

Jefferson did not speak during the long debate, but sat quietly, taking notes as each speaker made his points in turn. When Congress postponed final debate until July 1, Jefferson still had not spoken a word on the wisdom of declaring American independence. But he did not go unnoticed.

On June 11 Congress named a committee to draft a declaration to explain to Americans and to the world at large why the colonies sought independence. After the declaration was ready, Congress would vote whether to adopt it. Thomas Jefferson was named to the committee despite his youth and despite his silence in Congress. John Adams had persuaded many members to vote for Jefferson because of his "reputation for literature, science, and a happy talent of composition." Adams had read some of Jefferson's

The disagreements in Congress reflected life in a deeply divided America. As shown in this drawing, patriots and Tories sometimes handled one another roughly.

other writings and admired their "peculiar felicity of expression."
And by now he and Jefferson had become good friends. "Though
a silent member in Congress," Adams wrote of the Virginian, "he
was so prompt, frank, explicit and decisive upon committees and
in conversation . . . that he soon seized upon my heart."

Other members of this important committee, most of whom
favored independence, were John Adams of Massachusetts, Benjamin Franklin of Pennsylvania, Roger Sherman of Connecticut,
and Robert R. Livingston of New York. The five met at once and
Jefferson was chosen to write the document. Long afterward Jefferson recalled that the committee "unanimously pressed" him to
undertake the draft. "I consented, I drew it."

In his old age John Adams had a different memory. He and
Jefferson were named as a subcommittee, Adams said. At their
first meeting Jefferson said:

"You should make the draft."

"No, I will not," Adams replied. "You shall do it."

"Why?"

"Reasons enough," said Adams. "First, you are a Virginian, and
a Virginian ought to appear at the head of this business. Second,
I am obnoxious, suspected and unpopular; you are very much
otherwise. Third, you can write ten times better than I can."

"Well," Jefferson said, "if you are decided, I will do as well as
I can."

"Very well, when you have drawn it up we will have a meeting."

Jefferson retired to his rooms in Jacob Graff's house and began
work, writing and rewriting with many painstaking revisions. His
only guide was the brief recommendation of the committee: "I
turned to neither book nor pamphlet while writing it." But he was
prepared by a lifetime of reading and study that had begun even
before he had entered the College of William and Mary in Williamsburg. Jefferson had especially steeped himself in the works of
philosophers who wrote of the rights of free men—ancient writers
like Aristotle and Cicero, modern writers like John Locke and
Montesquieu.

Within two days Jefferson had drafted the Declaration of Independence which was to make him famous. The ideas he used had never before been so forcefully and clearly expressed. Though they were not new, they now had a freshness and power which moved all who read the Declaration.

Jefferson realized from the start that he faced a difficult task in justifying Lee's resolution for independence. He had to prepare an inspired piece of writing of a kind never seen before. It must be lucid and logical, yet impassioned—a plea for understanding for the Revolution. It must be written not for scholars and politicians alone, but for the plain people of his day and those who were to come after them.

He made no pretense of originality. The important task, he said, was "not to find out new principles, or new arguments, never before thought of, not merely to say things that had never been said before; but to place before mankind the common sense of the subject, in terms so plain and firm as to command their assent and to justify ourselves in the independent stand. . . . Neither aiming at originality . . . nor yet copied from any particular and previous writing, it was intended to be an expression of the American mind."

Only a few days earlier Jefferson had read the new Virginia Declaration of Rights, written by George Mason:

> All men are by nature equally free and independent, and have certain inherent rights, of which when they enter into a state of society, they cannot, by any compact, deprive or divest their posterity; namely, the enjoyment of life and liberty, with the means of acquiring and possessing property, and pursuing and obtaining happiness and safety.

Daring words, but they lacked the ring of those by Jefferson written in solitude in his furnished parlor, on his portable writing box.

The corresponding words of the Declaration, after slight changes by other Congressmen, have a power all their own:

> We hold these truths to be self-evident; that all men are created
> equal; that they are endowed by their Creator with certain un-
> alienable rights; that among these are life, liberty and the pursuit
> of happiness. . . .

The Declaration was the greatest writing of Jefferson's life. It
was an almost perfect union of political ideals and patriot propaganda—all so beautifully expressed that it is still regarded as a
model of writing. The cadence of its style is peculiarly Jefferson's
and it is marked by noble, unforgettable phrases.

When he had completed his rough draft of the document, Jefferson took it to John Adams, who suggested two minor changes
and made a copy for himself. The Declaration went next to Benjamin Franklin, who was suffering from gout and was unable to
attend sessions of Congress. Franklin made five changes. On June
28, just seventeen days after the committee was named, the Declaration was presented to Congress. By now, twenty-six changes
had been made in the original, the two by Adams, the five by
Franklin—and sixteen by Jefferson himself, who continued to
polish his work until it went off to the printer. There were also
three new paragraphs added by Jefferson.

Congress postponed voting on the Declaration until after voting
on Lee's resolution. Debate began on July 1. The day brought
another fierce clash between the opposing factions. Each of the
thirteen colonies had one vote. The Maryland legislature had
changed its mind and directed its delegates to vote for independence. The New York members said that though they approved of
independence and thought their people approved, they were forbidden to vote for it because of last year's instructions. By the end
of the day's debate nine colonies favored independence, South
Carolina and Pennsylvania voted no, Delaware's two delegates
were divided, and New York was forced to abstain.

The hesitation of some delegates was understandable. Men who signed this document would become not only rebels but—if their war was lost—traitors as well. They stood to lose everything, their homes, their property, perhaps their lives.

Rutledge of South Carolina gave the rebel leaders hope by saying that his delegation might change its mind overnight. Congress adjourned.

The next day, July 2, the vote was finally taken. South Carolina had changed to a yes vote. The third member from Delaware arrived and cast his vote for independence. Seven Pennsylvania delegates who arrived late outvoted Dickinson and Wilson. Except for the vote of New York, which still abstained, the vote in favor of independence was unanimous.

The daring step had been taken! It remained only to approve the Declaration which explained the resolution—and then, somehow, to win the war itself.

For two days Congress debated Jefferson's document word by word. The author sat by, squirming uncomfortably as other members made changes in his work—"mutilations" and "depredations," he called them. No one kept an exact record of the debate, and there are differences in the several original copies of the Declaration still in existence. So many details of the changes are unknown. Others are obvious.

Jefferson had charged the English people, as well as King George III, with making war on Americans. Some Congressmen insisted that this charge be struck out. This enraged Jefferson, who scorned "the pusillanimous idea that we had friends in England worth keeping terms with." He had also denounced the King's use of "Scotch and other foreign auxiliaries" as troops in the colonies. But Congressmen of Scottish origin protested, and these words were removed. Congress eliminated whole paragraphs, marking out passages which denounced the King too strongly. The whole manuscript was shortened to make its meaning clearer. Jefferson had not thought it proper to call upon God in this political docu-

ment, but Congress inserted in several places the words "God" and "Divine Providence."

A major change in the Declaration, one which bore the seeds of future American tragedy, was the elimination of a paragraph denouncing the King for defending the cruel and immoral slave trade. "Southern gentlemen" had this removed, Jefferson said, aided by Northern Congressmen whose consciences were heavy because of their own part in the business of human slavery. Jefferson's hatred of slavery was genuine enough, and he was not without supporters. But it was clear that if this passage were left in the Declaration, Congress would be split and a union of the colonies would be impossible.

At last, on July 4, the wrangling was over. Representatives of

New Yorkers—black, white, and Indian—helped to pull down the King's statue after the Declaration of Independence.

twelve colonies (with New York casting no ballot) agreed to the Declaration as it stood.

On that evening, after the rash of final changes, the Declaration went to a printer—and took its place as one of the most remarkable documents in history. Celebrations began immediately as word spread through the country. It was not until August 2 that the Declaration was officially placed in Congressional records and members began signing their names. Even then fifteen members were missing, and the last of them did not sign until November.

John Adams wrote in a letter to his wife: "Yesterday the greatest question was decided which ever was debated in America, and a greater, perhaps, never was nor will be decided among men. . . . It will be celebrated by succeeding generations as the great anniversary festival. It ought to be solemnized with pomp and parade, with shows, games, sports, guns, bells, bonfires and illuminations, from one end of this continent to the other, from this time forward forevermore."

Jefferson sent copies of his original to several friends, so that they could see how his work had been changed. Some of them wrote back in sympathy—but agreed that the final effect was superb. Richard Henry Lee wrote, "I wish sincerely, as well for the honor of Congress, as for that of the States, that the Manuscript had not been mangled as it is. However the Thing is in its nature so good, that no Cookery can spoil the Dish for the palates of Freemen."

After all, despite alterations, it was Jefferson's work. Years later, when his wounded pride had healed, the author looked back upon it as one of the great achievements of his long and useful life. Later historians concluded that for all the haste and the necessity for compromise, Congress had improved upon the rough draft of the Declaration. The revisions left it clearer, stronger, and more persuasive, a model of inspired thought expressed in plain, forceful language.

Jefferson's great work in Philadelphia was done. He remained in Congress a few weeks longer. But on September 3 he left for Monticello, his fine house on a hilltop near Charlottesville, Virginia, which he was to spend forty years in building and renovating. He soon went to Williamsburg as an Assembly delegate. There he helped to change the rigid laws of Virginia, making the old colony into a more democratic society. As he said, he "laid the ax to the root of pseudo-aristocracy."

Virginia's wealthy conservatives were outraged. Landon Carter complained that Jefferson must be "a midday drunkard" to propose such schemes, and said that he was depriving men of "the right to do as we please with our property." Jefferson also rewrote laws on crime and punishment, on religion and education. He made brilliant and revolutionary proposals. One was for a system of free public education throughout Virginia. Each year each school would send a poor boy of "best genius" to a higher school on a scholarship, and the ten finest scholars in the state would be sent to the College of William and Mary for three years. It was the first complete state school system to be proposed in America.

Jefferson continued to fight slavery. "Nothing is more certainly written in the book of fate than that these people are to be free," he wrote. "I tremble for my country when I reflect that God is Just."

He entered the bitterest fight of his life in an attempt to pass a law for religious freedom, overthrowing old laws which required support of the established church by all citizens. Conservative Virginians defeated his efforts for many years—as they did his proposals for education and prison reform. But Jefferson lived to see many of his dreams realized in the granting of new rights to Virginians and to all Americans.

In the last years of the Revolution he served as Virginia's second governor. It was a frustrating time, in which he tried in vain to resist British invasions and to strengthen a weak new government under which few men seemed willing to make sacrifices for the public good. He once narrowly escaped capture by the British in a cavalry raid on Monticello.

Though a brilliant career lay ahead of him as Minister to France, Secretary of State, Vice President, President, and founder of the University of Virginia, he had already made his great contribution to the Revolution and the cause of free men everywhere. Among all the works of his life, he was to be remembered chiefly as the author of the Declaration of Independence, whose influence was to be felt in many nations. In his old age Jefferson wrote of his work during those hot days of June in Philadelphia: "The flames kindled on the 4th of July, 1776, have spread over too much of the globe to be extinguished by the feeble engines of despotism; on the contrary, they will consume these engines and all who work them."

Thomas Paine

Radical Pamphleteer

In the dim glow of a campfire near the village of Newark, New Jersey, a frail little man huddled against the cold wind, writing on fluttering sheets which he held on the head of an army drum. It was November 1776, and the Revolution was nineteen months old. George Washington's army was straggling in retreat across New Jersey. Its cause seemed hopeless, and the well-fed, well-armed British army invincible. The ragged Americans in camp were ready to give up, and Congress had fled from Philadelphia to Baltimore.

The face of the earnest little man revealed the passion with which he wrote, more hurriedly now. The words he scrawled were soon to sweep the country, revive the patriot cause, and give Washington and his disheartened men courage to launch a surprise attack on the enemy.

The writer, an aide to General Nathanael Greene, was a newspaperman from Philadelphia named Thomas Paine. He was pale, thin, withdrawn, a man who drew little attention in a crowd. But,

Washington's troops crossing the icy Delaware. The scene was painted by a Marblehead artist, proud of the Massachusetts fishermen who rowed the boats.

as John Adams said, he had "genius in his eyes." Paine called his new pamphlet *The Crisis,* and its opening phrases were to ring like a bugle call through the colonies:

> These are the times that try men's souls. The summer soldier and the sunshine patriot will, in this crisis, shrink from the service of their country; but he that stands it *now,* deserves the love and thanks of man and woman. Tyranny, like hell, is not easily conquered; yet we have this consolation with us, that the harder the conflict, the more glorious the triumph.

The rapid sentences flowed on, page after page, to the end:

> By perseverance and fortitude we have the prospect of a glorious issue; by cowardice and submission, the sad choice of a variety of evils—a ravaged country—a depopulated city—habitations without safety, and slavery without hope.

George Washington was deeply impressed by these words. He had them read aloud to his troops before they crossed the ice-choked Delaware on Christmas night, to attack the unsuspecting enemy garrison in Trenton. The thrilling words were still fresh in their minds as the men struggled across the river in a howling

The·TIMES are
Dreadful,
Difmal
Doleful
Dolorous, and
DOLLAR-LESS.

An Emblem of the Effects of the STAMP

O! the fatal Stam

Thurfday, *October* 31, 1765.

THE

NUMB. 1195.

PENNSYLVANIA JOURNAL;

AND

WEEKLY ADVERTISER.

EXPIRING: In Hopes of a Refurrection to LIFE again.

When Paine became editor of The Pennsylvania Journal, *the news-paper was already known for its support of the patriot cause. An earlier editor used skulls-and-crossbones in bitter protest against the Stamp Act.*

storm. Within a few weeks the pamphlet was known to almost every American. The New York Revolutionary Convention, which had dwindled to nine members, took heart and was revived. Deserters in other colonies returned to the army. *The Crisis* gave the discouraged young nation a new spirit.

As the war dragged on, Paine wrote sixteen more *Crisis* papers, dealing with each new threat to the rebel cause—a rumored plot of army officers to replace Washington, a British move to make trouble between the French and Americans, a proposal to make peace on terms favorable to England. When lack of money slowed the war effort, Paine asked wryly, "whether it is better to raise two millions to defend the country and govern it ourselves . . . or pay six millions to have it conquered and let the enemy govern it?"

As a boy Thomas Paine, son of a poor Quaker corset-maker in England, had only brief though useful schooling in his home town of Thetford. At the age of thirteen he went to work for his father as a stay-maker. But within three years Thomas ran away to sea

and served as a sailor on a British privateer in the war with France.
He returned to London to become a clerk in a tax office. He began
to educate himself in the belief that "every person of learning is
finally his own teacher." He saved money to buy books and globes
and other scientific equipment, and he attended lectures by
scholars.

Paine was drawn into the struggle to help poor English working
people. He was strongly moved by the sight of crowds in London,
"ragged and hungry children, and persons of seventy and eighty,
begging in the streets."

Thomas began writing in protest and was dismissed from his
government job as a troublemaker. To escape being jailed for
debt, he had to sell everything he owned. In 1774 he sailed for
Philadelphia to make a new life in America. Through the aid of
Benjamin Franklin, who gave him a letter of introduction, Paine
became editor of *The Pennsylvania Journal.*

As tension between England and America grew, he wrote elo-
quently in favor of independence. But he wanted more than freedom from Great Britain for his new countrymen. He wanted a
democracy, a complete change "from the monarchial to the repub-
lican form of government." Opposition was powerful, for many
wealthy Americans preferred British rule to the dangers of a democratic revolution.

Paine attacked these men in *The Pennsylvania Journal,* calling
for independence at once. He also condemned England for having
"employed herself in the most horrid of all traffics, that of human
flesh . . . and ravaged the hapless shore of Africa, robbing it of its
unoffending inhabitants to cultivate her stolen dominions in the
west." Thus Paine was not only insisting upon a break with England months before the Declaration of Independence. He was also
attacking slavery in America almost a century before the cruel
practice came to an end.

Paine soon showed a new manuscript to two of his influential
Philadelphia friends, Dr. Benjamin Rush and David Rittenhouse.

Rush suggested a title—*Common Sense*—and the pamphlet appeared in January 1776. It was a call for a free America, the first of modern republics, with the power of government to be held by the people. Paine foresaw the future role of the United States:

> O! Ye that love mankind! Ye that dare oppose not only the tyranny but the tyrant, stand forth! Every spot of the old world is overrun with oppression. Freedom hath been hunted around the globe. Asia and Africa have long expelled her. Europe regards her like a stranger, and England hath given her warning to depart. O! receive the fugitive, and prepare in time for an asylum for mankind.

Common Sense, published anonymously, was a sensation. Soon half a million copies were in print. Thousands of Americans quoted its phrases. Even conservative colonial leaders were swayed by this pamphlet. George Washington wrote, "A few more of such flaming arguments as . . . the sound doctrine and unanswerable reasoning of *Common Sense* will not leave numbers at a loss to decide upon the propriety of a separation." He added later, "I find that *Common Sense* is working a powerful change in the minds of many men."

Common Sense was a simple, forceful document on the nature of man and government. "There is something exceedingly ridiculous in the composition of monarchy," wrote Paine. "The state of a King shuts him from the world, yet the business of a King requires him to know it thoroughly." Paine attacked George III as a "hardened sullen-tempered Pharaoh" and the "Royal Brute of Great Britain." In a day when men could hardly imagine government without kings, these lines were exciting reading for the subjects of a powerful monarch.

Paine realized that the fighting in Massachusetts and the debates in the legislature of Virginia were both parts of one vital cause. " 'Tis not in numbers but in unity that our great strength lies,"

THOMAS PAINE.

Paine continued. "No single colony is able to support itself, and the whole, when united, is able to do any thing!"

Thomas Paine was more devoted to the revolutionary cause than many native-born Americans. Despite his poverty, he donated to the revolutionary movement all money from the sale of *Common Sense,* and he added the small fortune of $2500 voted him by the legislature of Pennsylvania.

Tory leaders, stunned by the effects of the pamphlet, wrote newspaper attacks against the "artful, insidious and pernicious" tract. But public demand for independence grew stronger. And Paine's writings had a direct influence on the writing of the Declaration of Independence in July 1776. Jefferson said that he embraced "the same principles" of which Paine wrote, and paid tribute to the Englishman's skill. "No writer had exceeded Paine in ease and familiarity of style," said Jefferson, "and in simple and unassuming language."

Paine later helped to obtain a radical constitution for Pennsylvania, written largely by his friend Benjamin Franklin. Judges were to be elected, not appointed. Most men could vote, not just well-to-do property owners. The legislature had only one house, so that no smaller, aristocratic upper house could offset the power of a larger, more democratic lower house. The new constitution destroyed aristocratic rule in Pennsylvania. It was a pattern that Jefferson was to follow in Virginia, and it changed American life for all time by making it more democratic.

After the battle of Trenton, where *The Crisis* helped to inspire the American victory, Paine became a kind of public-relations man for Washington's tattered forces. Washington and other leaders persuaded Congress to vote Paine a salary of $800 a year to continue to arouse the public and keep alive the spirit of rebellion. Paine also held several government positions. As Congressional secretary to the Committee on Foreign Affairs, he helped to obtain loans and military assistance from France for the rebels.

Near the end of the war, state jealousies were endangering passage of the Articles of Confederation, a first step toward permanent union. Maryland refused to sign the Articles until Virginia gave up her claims to the Northwest Territory, which blocked western settlements by Maryland and Pennsylvania. Paine attacked Virginia's claims in a pamphlet called *Public Good,* insisting that the western lands had been won by the national war effort, and that Americans should work for unity and forget state pride. Virginia deeded the lands to the United States and the way was opened to form the American union.

At the end of the Revolution, when Paine was poverty-stricken, Congress refused to help him. But two states came to his aid, Pennsylvania granting him $500 in cash and New York a farm near New Rochelle.

Paine traveled to France just as the French people opened a revolution of their own to reform the regime of King Louis XVI. The French were strongly influenced by the American Revolution. As a link between the two, Paine was greeted in Paris as a hero. To help this new cause Paine wrote one of his greatest pamphlets, *The Rights of Man*.

When the French radicals executed the King and many of the nobility, Paine protested bitterly. He was thrown into prison, from which he was rescued many months later by the American Minister, James Monroe. In 1802, at the invitation of President Jefferson, Paine returned to the United States, where he continued his writing.

He was popular with common people who remembered his services in the Revolution. But he was scorned by many Americans because of his pamphlets attacking the narrow-minded church leaders of his time. He was branded an atheist, "a loathsome reptile," a "demi-human archbeast," a "lying, drunken, brutal infidel." Only a few old friends, like Thomas Jefferson and the inventor Robert Fulton, remained loyal to him. Paine died in a rooming house on Fulton Street in New York City on June 8, 1809, and was buried on his farm in New Rochelle. A few years later his bones were dug up and carried to England.

For many years Paine was forgotten by "respectable" Americans. It was almost the middle of the twentieth century before his reputation was revived and the importance of his creed once more excited men who believed in freedom for everyone:

"My country is the world; to do good, my religion."

Benjamin Franklin

Master of Diplomacy

The American armed sloop *Reprisal,* driven by wild December gales, slipped into harbor on the coast of Brittany near the end of the year 1776. Three passengers went ashore—a stout, balding, gout-ridden old man wearing a coonskin hat, and his two grandsons, aged seven and sixteen. Benjamin Franklin, a few days short of his seventy-first birthday, was invading France in search of aid which might win American independence.

The newcomers were met by astonished Breton peasants in broad-brimmed hats and baggy trousers, chattering in a tongue the Americans could not interpret. But Franklin soon made himself understood and, leaning heavily on his grandsons, clambered into a crude country coach and was off on a jolting ride to Paris. From the harbor, the *Reprisal* fired a farewell salute.

The old man had begun a mission that was to keep him in France for nine years while the war for freedom raged in his home country. He had come willingly. When Congress appointed him

Commissioner to Paris, Franklin said, "I am old and good for nothing. But, as the storekeepers say of their remnants of cloth, I am but a fag end, and you may have me for what you please."

He had given Congress all of his accumulated cash as a loan. He had worked with Thomas Paine on a radical new constitution for Pennsylvania. And he left behind in an American prison his only son, who had lately served as the Tory governor of New Jersey.

Franklin was the most famous American. He was known everywhere as an author, as a scientist, and as an inventor. In Europe he was widely believed to have organized the American Revolution and to have written the Declaration of Independence, *Common Sense,* and all other well-known American political documents.

Paris received him with open arms. He appeared at the court of King Louis XVI and Queen Marie Antoinette in plain brown Quaker garb, topped by the fur cap suggesting the American frontier, wearing spectacles of his own invention. His manner was calm and reserved, his expression wise and benign. Philosophers, court favorites, businessmen, and politicians were quickly won by the sage from the New World.

In his guise of a simple backwoodsman, Franklin began secret maneuvers in an effort to draw the French regime into the war as America's ally. An alliance would mean everything to the rebels. They could not hope for victory without help from abroad. Franklin was to have the temporary assistance of other Commissioners sent by Congress, including John Adams. But as the unofficial leader and recognized genius of the delegation, Franklin bore the main weight of the heavy diplomatic burden.

He began by talking to the Foreign Minister, the Comte de Vergennes. Franklin persuaded Vergennes that his old enemies, the English, would become all-powerful if they defeated the American rebels. To French merchants and shippers Franklin pictured the rich trade which would open with America once the British monopoly was broken. To the French philosophers, to men and women of the court, and to young nobles of liberal intellectual circles, Franklin spoke of the ideals of liberty for Americans—and for all men.

Official France was interested but cautious. Vergennes realized that his countrymen were already playing a dangerous game. They were sending secret aid to the American rebels—muskets, powder, uniforms, and food, shipped to the West Indies to be picked up by swift rebel schooners. The Foreign Minister was eager for revenge against England, which had humiliated France and seized her North American colonies. But he dared not risk an open alliance as long as the American cause seemed so hopeless. Washington's army had been defeated time and time again by the well-trained redcoats. Within a few days, however, Franklin got a promise of 2,000,000 francs in aid.

Franklin avoided the threats and intrigues suggested by his fellow Commissioners. He played a patient waiting game, and often behaved as if diplomacy was the least of his concerns.

Franklin attended the French Academy of Sciences, visited the great libraries of the city, and exchanged scientific and philosophical views with leading European scholars. His standing as a world figure led to close friendships with powerful French families, among them the Noailles clan. One member of this family, the Marquis de Lafayette, Franklin encouraged to sail for America. The 20-year-old Lafayette was to become one of Washington's most trusted officers and to play a major role in drawing France into the war. Franklin was besieged by other Europeans, such as Friedrich von Steuben, who longed to take part in the Revolution.

Franklin attacked England in sharply worded pamphlets which appeared without his name and became a sensation in many countries. One was "Comparison of Great Britain and the United States in regard to the basis of credit in the two countries," which contrasted England's enormous public debt with the rich resources and thrifty policies of America. The French were impressed by the promise of the new and undeveloped country as Franklin described it, and public opinion became strongly pro-American.

Young Lafayette became a major general under George Washington at the age of 23. Like his friend Benjamin Franklin, Lafayette worked tirelessly to bring France into the war as an ally.

French snuffbox decorated with a picture of Benjamin Franklin wearing spectacles and a frontiersman's fur hat.

Another pamphlet, a masterpiece of propaganda, was supposed to be a letter from a German prince who had hired out thousands of young Hessian soldiers to England for the American war. The prince was to receive thirty guineas for each mercenary killed. Needing money to help pay for a season of opera at his court, he was anxious for high casualties:

> I am about to send to you some new recruits. Don't economize them. Remember glory before all things. Glory is true wealth. There is nothing degrades the soldier like the love of money. He must care only for honour and reputation, but this reputation must be acquired in the midst of dangers. A battle gained without costing the conqueror any blood is an inglorious success, while the conquered cover themselves with glory by perishing with their arms in their hands. Do you remember that of the 300 Lacedaemonians who defended the defile of Thermopylae, not one returned? How happy should I be could I say the same of my brave Hessians!

The pamphlet made a deep impression in Paris and other European cities, where there was already resentment of the shipment of young Hessians to America as if they were cattle. The men were paid a few pennies a day while their rulers grew rich. These hired soldiers were important to the British, for the war in America was unpopular. At least one British regiment mutinied on the docks and refused to sail until they were disarmed and driven aboard ship.

Franklin became the darling of Parisian society. Women found him fascinating despite his age. He was said to have played chess with one friend, Madame Brillon, while she was in her bathtub. The old man had now become a national fad. His picture was seen everywhere, on rings and snuffboxes and lockets, and in frames over the fireplaces of homes throughout France. Franklin's likeness even appeared on chamber pots. He wrote his daughter Sally, "These pictures, busts and prints have made your father's face well known as that of the moon, so that he durst not do anything which would oblige him to run away." John Adams observed that Franklin was more admired than any famous man of the century, even the scientist Isaac Newton, or the statesman Frederick the Great, or the philosopher Voltaire:

> His name was familiar to government and people, to Kings, courtiers, nobility, clergy and philosophers, as well to plebians, to such a degree that there was scarcely a peasant or a citizen, a *valet de chambre,* coachman or footman, or a lady's chambermaid or a scullion in a kitchen who was not familiar with it and who did not consider him a friend to humankind. When they spoke of him they seemed to think that he would restore the golden age.

Despite such public acclaim, Franklin feared that he might be failing in his mission. For almost a year the French refused to enter the war lest the rebellion be soon crushed. News from America grew worse. The British recaptured Fort Ticonderoga. Then they occupied Philadelphia, putting Congress to flight.

An Englishman taunted Franklin, "Has Howe really taken Philadelphia?"

"No," said Franklin with a smile, "Philadelphia has taken Howe."

And when friends despaired of the crisis in America, Franklin said calmly, "It will pass."

His replies were repeated all over Paris. Though French admiration for him grew, ruin threatened America. General John Burgoyne was invading from Canada, pushing south to join General Howe, trap Washington's army, and cut New England off from the other colonies. France and Spain sent money to the

The war was not very popular in England. This cartoon reflects the reluctance of many British soldiers to fight against the determined rebels (background).

rebels, but suspected that the cause was lost. Franklin seemed to be helpless. British diplomats now began to feel out the Americans with peace offers.

At last, in December 1777, when he had been in France just a year, Franklin got news of the great American victory at Saratoga, in which Burgoyne's invading army had been captured. This defeat and capture of an entire British army of 5,000 men was a turning point of the Revolution. Franklin hurried the news to Vergennes and urged that France sign a treaty of alliance. Young King Louis was willing, but only if Spain would join him—and Spain refused.

But then Franklin hinted that the Americans and British might make peace. If this happened, there was a danger that the two would join in conquering French islands in the West Indies. So King Louis agreed to the treaty of alliance. He would not wait for Spain. He offered troops, ships, supplies, and weapons.

The news set off wild celebrations in America, where many thought that victory was near.

Franklin soon became the only American diplomat in France, with the title of Minister Plenipotentiary. For years he directed an endless flow of French aid to America. Finally, with the help of young General Lafayette, he persuaded the French to send 5,000 troops to assist George Washington's army.

In 1781, as the crisis of the Revolution approached, General Washington made a desperate call for more money, which Franklin helped to obtain. Conditions in the American army improved rapidly. The victory in October of that year was as much French as American. It could not have been won without men, arms, ships, and money sent from Paris—largely because of the persuasiveness of Benjamin Franklin.

War had always distressed Franklin. He wrote to an English friend, Edmund Burke, who favored the rebels:

> Since the foolish part of mankind will make wars . . . not having sense enough otherwise to settle their differences, it certainly becomes the wiser part, who cannot prevent these wars, to alleviate as much as possible the calamities attending them.

Congress named Franklin as one of four Peace Commissioners, and he finally pushed through a treaty with Great Britain late in 1783. Franklin played the major role throughout the difficult dealings with the British which dragged on for more than two years. When the peace treaty was signed at last, it was on terms he had suggested many months earlier. As soon as the treaty was signed, Franklin wrote to Congress:

> I am now entering my seventy-eighth year; public business has engrossed fifty of them; I wish now to be, for the little time I have left, my own master. If I live to see this peace concluded, I shall beg leave to remind Congress of their promise then to dismiss me.

To a friend he wrote, "We are now friends with England and with all mankind. May we never see another war! For in my opinion there was never a good war or a bad peace."

It was 1785 before the semi-invalid Franklin left for America. He had served the American cause in France for nine years. He departed on a litter given him by Queen Marie Antoinette. His French friends and neighbors stood about in a solemn farewell as he left, and many of them sobbed.

The work of the war years in France was Franklin's great contribution to the birth of the United States, but it was by no means his only one. In a sense his life had been given to enlightening and inspiring his countrymen and to encouraging their independence of spirit. His youthful rise from printer's devil to author, editor, and publisher was as well known as any nursery tale. His writings, especially *Poor Richard's Almanac* and the little essay on *The Way to Wealth*, became a part of American life. Franklin's lively epigrams were so popular that they were embedded in folklore, like, "Early to bed, and early to rise, makes a man healthy, wealthy, and wise."

As an inventor, Franklin changed American life with his Franklin stove, his electrical experiments (including the development of the first storage battery), the odometer (to measure distances traveled by wagons and carriages), and an ingenious chair-table, or writing desk. Other inventions poured from his workroom—a musical instrument called the glass harmonica, a "mystery clock" with concealed works, bifocal spectacles. He took air and water readings and charted the course of the Gulf Stream. He founded America's first scientific association, the American Philosophical Society. He studied most of the sciences known to his day and expanded many frontiers of knowledge.

He seldom failed to approach his work with humor. He once charged a young woman with static electricity so that her lips gave off an electrical shock when she was kissed by her startled sweetheart. Franklin refused to take patents on his inventions. Since he profited from inventions of others, he said he should be "glad of an opportunity to serve others by an invention of ours; and this we should do freely and generously."

As head of the colonial post office, he greatly increased its efficiency. He became Secretary of the colony of Pennsylvania. He devised effective night-watch and fire-fighting services for Philadelphia and founded the first subscription library in America.

As quarrels developed between Great Britain and America, Franklin played a leading role. He clarified the issues in pointed cartoons and prose. He published the first political cartoon in America, depicting the colonies in the form of a snake cut into pieces, with the legend "Join or Die" (as shown on pages 28–29). This was the earliest proposal for a United States.

When Parliament in 1765 imposed taxes on goods sold in America, Franklin was in London as a representative of Pennsylvania. He was to spend the next ten years there, working to improve relations between England and America. He opposed the new taxes, but thought the Stamp Act was important only because it placed new taxes on goods within the colonies themselves. The philosopher-statesman became an American hero when, with the aid of British merchants whose trade had been damaged, he persuaded Parliament to repeal the hated taxes. Toasts were drunk to Franklin in many American towns.

Paris peace talks. Benjamin West could not complete his painting of the Peace Commissioners because the British refused to cooperate. But West portrayed (from left) John Jay, John Adams, Benjamin Franklin, and Henry Laurens. At right is William Temple Franklin, secretary to the U.S. Commissioners, who first came to France with his grandfather at the age of 16.

Though he tried to prevent war, Franklin was a leader of the patriot cause for the next ten years. When he heard of the Boston Tea Party, Franklin proposed a compromise by offering to pay for the tea himself—if Britain would repeal the tea tax. From both sides of the Atlantic, officials asked Franklin in London to help settle the growing quarrel, but all of his efforts failed. Americans insisted upon nothing less than self-government, and the British government would not yield. Franklin sailed for home in 1775 and was at sea when the fighting at Lexington and Concord opened the war that Franklin had so long sought to avert.

Franklin joined Congress as its oldest member. He was also one of the most active—as Postmaster General, designer and supervisory printer of Continental currency, and a director of the manufacture of gunpowder. With Thomas Jefferson and John Adams he designed the seal of the United States.

Like George Washington, Franklin seldom made speeches from the floor. This was not surprising, since his Poor Richard had said, "Here comes the orator, with his flood of words and his drop of wisdom." Thomas Jefferson later said that he never heard Franklin or Washington speak for as long as ten minutes, yet "they laid their shoulders to the great points, knowing that the little ones would follow of themselves." But John Adams, who constantly made fiery speeches, forcing delegates toward independence, did not admire Franklin. He said that the Pennsylvania sage slept in his chair much of the time.

Franklin worked furiously, despite his age and poor health. He devised defenses for the Delaware River to protect Philadelphia. He proposed a confederation of the colonies which Congress rejected. He went to Cambridge to inspect Washington's army, and he proposed a permanent military organization. Most important of all, he headed the Committee of Correspondence, which dealt with foreign governments and sought allies for the rebels. Franklin's hundreds of prominent friends in other countries made his task easier. For several months he conducted the first American

"Department of State." Six months before Congress had even considered the step, Franklin assured the French that Congress would declare American independence. He also bombarded his English friends with eloquent letters in an effort to gain popular support in Britain. After the battle of Bunker Hill he wrote the British scientist Joseph Priestley:

> Britain, at the expense of three millions has killed one hundred and fifty Yankees . . . which is twenty thousand pounds a head. . . . During the same time sixty thousand children have been born in America.

In late June 1776, when the Declaration of Independence was being written by Jefferson, Franklin made changes in the first draft, one of them a definite improvement. Jefferson had written, "We hold these truths to be sacred and undeniable." Franklin drew a line through the final three words and inserted "self-evident."

As the Declaration was signed Franklin made a grim joke—at least according to tradition. John Hancock said as he signed his name, "We must be unanimous; there must be no pulling in different ways; we must all hang together." Franklin is said to have quipped, "Yes, we must indeed all hang together or most assuredly we shall hang separately."

Only a few months later, chosen by Congress as the one American ideally suited for the task, Franklin was on his way to France, where he spent the war years in winning and holding the alliance which brought final victory. When he returned home, he was almost eighty. He was given a hero's welcome and was soon appointed to head the Executive Council of Pennsylvania.

He continued to work on his inventions. He designed a mechanical hand to reach books from tall shelves, a chair that opened to become a stepladder, and a cooling fan that worked with the touch of a foot.

But he was soon caught up in public affairs once more, and played a vital role in persuading the squabbling new states to accept the U.S. Constitution. Franklin suggested the compromises which brought the smaller and the larger states into agreement: The House of Representatives would be based on population (at first, one member for each 40,000 inhabitants) but every state would have two votes in the Senate.

Long after the war, when Washington had been inaugurated as the first President, Franklin wrote him: "For my own personal case I should have died two years ago; but . . . I am pleased that I have lived them, since they have brought me to see our present situation." The old man was forced to stop work on his autobiography before it was complete, but Franklin seemed to be fully prepared for death. A few days before the end he got out of bed and asked that it be made up for him so that he could "die in a decent manner."

His daughter said, "I hope you'll recover and live for many more years."

Franklin replied simply, "I hope not."

He died on April 17, 1790, at eighty-four, mourned by his countrymen and countless others elsewhere, one of the architects of world freedom as well as American freedom. He was the only man to sign the four great documents which brought the United States to life—the Declaration of Independence, the treaties with France and England, and the United States Constitution.

Friedrich von Steuben

The Drillmaster

George Washington's miserable troops welcomed a striking party of strangers to Valley Forge one day in February 1778. In a sleigh, with an Italian greyhound at his side, was a hard-faced Prussian officer in a new buff-and-blue uniform. Around him, in a carriage and on horseback, were five grooms and drivers, three servants, a cook, and three French aides. Only one of the party spoke English.

The stout officer clambered from the sleigh and stamped on the frozen earth. He stared at the rows of huts, from which the heads of American soldiers appeared, croaking their protests, "No bread, no soldier!"

Decorations blazed on the German's chest, among them the star of the Order of Baden, a symbol of knighthood. He called himself Baron Friedrich von Steuben, lieutenant general, former aide to Frederick the Great, the King of Prussia. And he was traveling with the aid of John Hancock of Massachusetts, who had provided him with the sleigh, carriage, servants, and uniforms. The baron,

Friedrich von Steuben.

one of Europe's leading military experts, according to himself, had come to make Washington's rabble into an army.

He found an army almost beyond hope. One company had shrunk from a hundred men to only one, a corporal. One regiment had only thirty men. The muskets were "in a horrible condition, covered with rust, half of them without bayonets," and many of them could not be fired. The men seemed to use their bayonets only for cooking meat over campfires. The baron was shocked at the sight of Washington's soldiers. "The men were literally naked," he observed. "The officers who had coats, had them of every color . . . made of an old blanket or a woolen bedcover. With regard to their military discipline, I may safely say no such thing existed."

This was not truly a national army, but a band of troops from every state, each fiercely independent. The soldiers made comic attempts at drill, each regiment following a system of its own. Many officers, as well as many enlisted men, had gone home for the winter. Each regiment camped as its colonel wished, without system or order. There were more supply officers than in all the armies of Europe. But no one kept track of arms, equipment, clothing, or ammunition. Men who had completed their service carried home their clothing and weapons. Quartermasters were paid a percentage of all money they spent for supplies, so that there was great waste—which added to the inflation of the new country's unstable currency.

Steuben marveled that the army had hung together. No European army would have done so under such conditions. But his heart sank as he made his first inspection of the camp. "My determination," he said later, "must have been very firm that I did not abandon my design when I saw the troops."

Steuben was a kind of fraud, with only a shaky claim to the title of baron. He was not a lieutenant general but a retired captain in the Prussian army. He had served as his King's aide—but not

American soldiers trying to get warm at Valley Forge.

in the important way he pretended. He was, instead, a poor adventurer, heavily in debt.

But in Paris he had convinced Benjamin Franklin, who realized that the "baron" was just such a soldier as the infant American army needed. Armed with letters of praise from France, Steuben crossed the Atlantic. He deceived Congress and General Washington—fortunately for the American cause—and received the rank of Inspector General of the Continental Army. He turned out to be a fine drillmaster who made soldiers out of a band of half-trained nomads. The baron was to play a prominent part in American victory, for without him the underfed, underpaid troops would have lacked discipline to endure the long war.

George Washington was eager for the kind of help Steuben could give, for the Commander in Chief had always wanted a professional army rather than a loose-knit band of guerrillas. Until now, no officer of the Continental Army had been qualified to teach tactics and field maneuvers. Washington, Greene, Knox, and most other American generals were self-taught soldiers, without professional training. In full-scale battle the army was difficult to handle. It straggled across country in single file, and when it was in motion stretched for many miles, so that it could not be quickly concentrated. Until now, the only battle training had been in combat itself.

The army's transportation was cumbersome and its supply of food was a farce. Inefficient supply was largely responsible for the grim conditions at Valley Forge, while in Philadelphia, a few miles away, the well-organized British troops were well fed and comfortable.

Despite his relief at Steuben's arrival on this cold February day, Washington greeted the German cautiously. He had been disappointed too often by European officers who flocked to his army, and he had become wary of foreign adventurers. Within a few days, however, Steuben won him over.

The Prussian wasted no time. Within three months, when spring brought fighting weather, he must teach the troops to maneuver and fight. He saw at once that he could not drill these soldiers as he had drilled his Prussians, so he worked day and night to develop a new system for the Americans. Steuben had no false pride. He became a drill instructor himself—a general doing the duty of a sergeant. Officers and men who went to the parade ground to see him at work were soon won by the general's modesty and enthusiasm.

Steuben trained an honor company of about a hundred experienced soldiers to serve as a model for the army. But at first he taught only one squad—eight or ten men. He rose at 3 A.M., had his pigtail braided by a German servant, drank his coffee, planned his day's work, and was out on the chilly drill field before six o'clock in full uniform. One soldier thought the general looked like Mars, the fierce god of Roman mythology:

> Never before, or since, have I had such an impression of the ancient fabled God of War as when I looked on the Baron . . . the trappings of his horse, the enormous holsters of his pistols, his large size, and his strikingly martial aspect.

The baron began to teach his squad the simplest lessons, first the "position of the soldier" at attention. He had learned a few

English words. But he taught the men largely by gestures, show-
ing them how to stand, how to "dress" right and left, how to take
slow marching steps. He went through each move himself, and
corrected the men as they imitated him. Soon they were following
him about the field, chanting the words he called in his heavy
accent: "VON-TWO-TREE-FOUR!"

The men worked until nightfall, repeated their lessons the following day, and went on to new movements. Hundreds of men
had soon learned the basic marching step and could move in disciplined ranks, even over rough open country. The baron divided
his company and sent instructors throughout the army, determined
to train all of Washington's regiments.

Next the men learned the manual of arms, so that all soldiers
would use their muskets and equipment in the same way, and all
could fire weapons with speed and skill. The baron then set the
army to learning the use of the bayonet, and the fields about Valley
Forge resounded with the clanging of steel. Americans overcame
their fear of the weapon and became confident that they were
ready to fight the British at close quarters.

When Steuben could not make himself understood, he splut-
tered helplessly in German, red-faced and angry. The troops
roared with laughter when he called upon his assistants to help
him swear. But they became fond of him, in spite of and because
of his peculiar ways. The drills continued. For the first time
American troops had proper training in war maneuvers, attacking
and defending positions, learning to change front and form ranks
under fire. Early in May, Washington held a review to show off
the army's new skills. Steuben directed a parade, field maneuvers,
and a spectacular show of musket firing. The soldiers behaved
like well-trained veterans.

An American officer who saw a British spy watching the display
ordered his men to let the spy return to the enemy. "The news of
this army today will be more painful to them than the loss of a
spy," he said. "Be sure that he is free to report all he has seen."

A scornful British view of American rebels early in the war.

At a dinner that evening, Washington announced a surprise—the new rank of major general for the baron. An officer wrote from Valley Forge:

> The Army grows stronger every day. It increases in number . . . and there is a spirit of discipline among the troops that is better than numbers. . . . The troops are instructed in a new method of marching so that they will soon be able to advance with the utmost regularity, even without music and on the roughest grounds.

After the terrible winter, it was a bright spring at Valley Forge. There was news of an alliance between France and the United States, with promises of French troops, ships, and supplies. And

Americaner Soldat.

An admiring German view of the American fighting man during the Revolution.

now the American army felt a new confidence. When the British army of Sir Henry Clinton marched from Philadelphia toward New York, exposing its long wagon train of supplies, Washington moved. Baron von Steuben was sent to scout the enemy. He found them marching toward Monmouth Courthouse, in New Jersey.

Washington's army attacked, and the Steuben-trained troops fought as Americans had seldom fought before. More than once they met the British veterans at bayonet point—and held their ground. Washington failed to destroy Clinton's army in the battle, but that may have been the fault of his erratic general, Charles Lee, and not of the troops themselves. They had clearly shown the value of their training during the long, hot day of battle.

Steuben's methods spread through the army and became permanent. Washington realized that Steuben had accomplished much during the winter. Steuben himself claimed proudly that he had brought order from chaos, despite all handicaps. He may have exaggerated his contribution, but it was clear that the army was much improved. Fewer than twenty muskets had been lost since he had taken over training, and Steuben estimated that he had saved the new nation millions of dollars a year.

Monmouth Courthouse was the last major clash of the armies in the Northern states. But even in the stalemate which followed, Steuben's methods proved invaluable to the Americans. The baron did much to hold together the army for the next two years.

The winter of 1780–81 was even more terrible than Valley Forge. But though the army suffered in its frozen camp at Morristown, New Jersey, the new discipline kept the regiments together despite incredible hardships. Even when one part of the army mutinied because of lack of pay, food, and shelter, the others remained loyal. And with the coming of another spring, they were eager for a decisive test against the British. A new French army had arrived in Newport, Rhode Island. It marched to join Washington near New York for a move into Virginia.

Before the troops began this march, Baron von Steuben was already in Virginia, aiding the young Marquis de Lafayette in his effort to prevent the escape of General Cornwallis. The baron found the South quite unlike the camp at Valley Forge. The Prussian veteran complained that Virginia civilians had little enthusiasm for the war, and he spoke out angrily against men who would not help to drive British invaders from their state. Once, when five hundred Virginia volunteers had promised to meet him at a country courthouse, the baron found only five men—three of whom then deserted.

The baron began to wish he had never seen the place. He wrote:

> I shall always regret that circumstances induced me to undertake the defense of a country where Caesar and Hannibal would have lost their reputation, and where every farmer is a general, but nobody wishes to be a soldier.

But the end of the war was near. In September 1781, when Washington and the French commander, the Comte de Rochambeau, arrived in Virginia with their armies, Steuben joined them at Williamsburg. Washington asked his advice about an attack against the British in nearby Yorktown and made him Inspector General of the army once more.

Steuben, like many other officers, was by now a pauper, ruined by inflation of American currency, as more and more of the almost worthless Continental bills poured from the presses. The baron was forced to ask Washington for a month's pay in coin, but was sadly refused. There was no hard cash in the army. Steuben sold some of his silver spoons in camp to feed one of his aides, who was ill.

When the battles of the Revolution were over, Steuben was almost penniless. If he had not drawn army rations like a common soldier and been fed by French officers, he would have gone hungry. He borrowed a handful of Portuguese coins from General Knox. And he was again forced to ask Washington for help, explaining that he could not live on his salary and that he was unable to collect money due him from Congress. The commander gave him money from his own purse.

Steuben tried for years to collect $8500 due him for his wartime services, but he was paid only $1700. It was five years after the war before Steuben was paid more. But he was also given a sword with a golden hilt, and a new city on the frontier was named for him, Steubenville, Ohio. Most important of all, the state of New York granted him 16,000 acres in the Mohawk Valley, where he settled in a log cabin, making plans to build a mansion.

Steuben never returned to his native Germany. He died in his cabin in 1794, at the age of sixty-four, his thoughts still with the ragged men of the Revolution whom he had made into soldiers, in the days when he had masqueraded as a lieutenant general. All had been forgiven. His old comrades knew that whatever false claims he had made when he came to Valley Forge, he had been the greatest of drillmasters, a teacher of the art of war who had done much to make the American victory possible.

George Rogers Clark

Conqueror of the West

The dark waters of the flooded river roared among the rocks, foaming through the rapids, a stretch of white water known as the Falls of the Ohio. The wilderness echoed with the river's subdued thunder. A dozen or more stout new boats manned by oarsmen in buckskins approached the rapids, and at that moment the river and the summer forest grew dark. As the first of the boats swept into the wild rush of the rapids, the shadow grew blacker. An eclipse of the sun had fallen upon the frontier. It was June 24, 1778.

In the boats were about 170 Kentuckians, off on a long, dangerous journey westward into the Illinois country, the stronghold of the British and their Indian allies. The boatmen were out to avenge raids which threatened to wipe out the settlements along the Kentucky frontier. The men were the troops of 25-year-old George Rogers Clark, a red-haired major of militia, who was leading one of the most daring expeditions in American history.

The grim men in his boats felt that they had little chance to re-

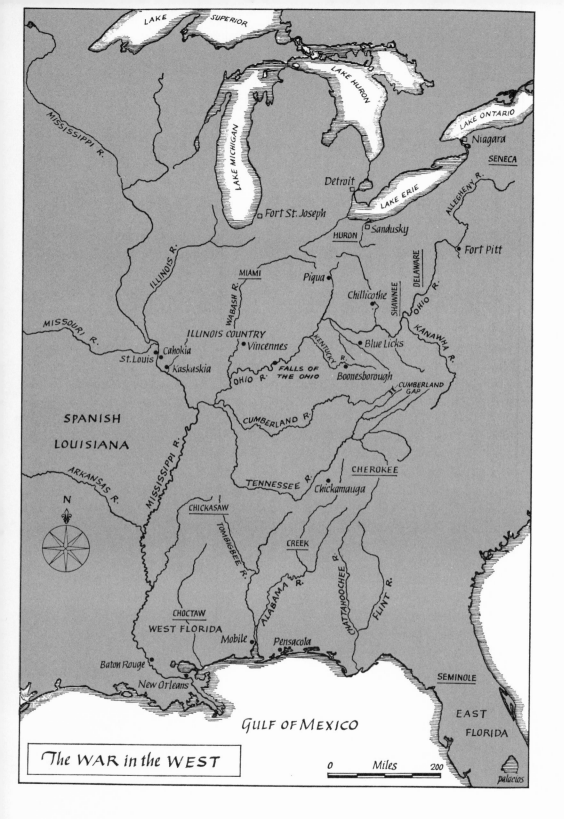

LAKE SUPERIOR

LAKE HURON

LAKE MICHIGAN

LAKE ONTARIO

● Niagara

SENECA

MISSISSIPPI R.

Detroit □

LAKE ERIE

ALLEGHENY R.

Fort St. Joseph □

● Sandusky

HURON

DELAWARE

● Fort Pitt

MIAMI

Piqua ●

OHIO R.

MISSOURI R.

WABASH R.

Chillicothe

SHAWNEE

KANAWHA R.

ILLINOIS COUNTRY

KENTUCKY R.

● Blue Licks

Cahokia ●

● Vincennes

St. Louis ●

OHIO R.

FALLS OF THE OHIO

Boonesborough ●

● Kaskaskia

CUMBERLAND GAP

SPANISH

LOUISIANA

CUMBERLAND R.

ARKANSAS R.

CHEROKEE

TENNESSEE R.

Chickamauga ●

N

CHICKASAW

MISSISSIPPI R.

CREEK

TOMBIGBEE R.

CHATTAHOOCHEE R.

ALABAMA R.

FLINT R.

CHOCTAW

WEST FLORIDA

Mobile ●

Pensacola ●

SEMINOLE

Baton Rouge ●

New Orleans

EAST

FLORIDA

GULF OF MEXICO

The WAR in the WEST

0   Miles   200

palacios

turn alive. But they would not turn back. They must either halt Indian raids on Kentucky or else give up their rich lands and retreat into Virginia. Behind them, Kentucky was swept by massacres, and many forts were in ashes. Daniel Boone himself had been besieged and wounded by Indian allies of the British. Hundreds of settlers had already streamed back eastward.

Only hours before, Clark had told his little band that they were bound down the Ohio. Their mission was to surprise enemy outposts along the Mississippi, capture a fort at Vincennes, and perhaps strike at British headquarters in Detroit itself:

> The tribes will never stop killing and burning until we take the war to them. We will strike at their villages, and drive out the British who lead them. It will not be easy, but we must march through the heart of Illinois country.

The Kentuckians understood. The Illinois country, which lay north and west of the Ohio, was territory few Americans dared to travel. Its river passages were controlled by village outposts the British had seized from the French during the French and Indian Wars many years before. The Frenchmen who still lived there were now British allies. Clark, who had already sent two scouts deep into this enemy-held territory, believed that the old French villages could be surprised and taken.

Clark and his men were determined to surprise and destroy these outposts, drive the Indian tribes from the war, and seize control of the whole territory from the British. In order to protect Kentucky and other frontier settlements, the major was opening a second front in the Revolution.

The British commander in the Northwest was Colonel Henry Hamilton, known as the "Hair Buyer" because he paid rewards for American scalps, even those of children. (Fighting men of both sides took scalps in the harsh frontier warfare.) Hamilton had called a council of 1600 Indian warriors in Detroit, where the braves heard British speeches and put on war paint. Hamilton had 900 troops at Detroit, many of them redcoat regulars; 1200 at the villages of Kaskaskia and Cahokia, on the Mississippi; and 250 more at Vincennes on the Wabash. Six British vessels commanded the Great Lakes. Thus Hamilton was master of the whole Northwest Territory, with allies among every large Indian tribe of the region. It seemed impossible that Clark could hope to oppose such force.

And yet, on this warm day in late June, Clark's men sped down the Ohio, leaving friendly settlements behind. Mile after mile they saw nothing but the edge of the wilderness—no cabin, no chimney smoke, no boat, no sign of the presence of man.

Though they were but a handful, Clark's troops carried with them the hopes of the American future. The Revolution might be won on the Atlantic coast by Washington and his Continental Army—and yet leave the British and their Indian allies in control of the Mississippi Valley. The skirmishes these men would fight in the wild country to the northwest might be as important as great battles between armies of many thousands in the east. Far away in New Jersey, Washington's army was preparing to fight the battle of Monmouth. The Commander in Chief was unaware that Clark and his men were off on an adventure that would secure the frontier.

The men who swept down the Ohio knew little about the war in the east. They knew only that Major Clark was a man they could trust, and that they must fight to save their homes and families in Kentucky. Some were uneasy until the shadow of the eclipse passed away, but the braver men were as eager as their leader for sight of the enemy.

The band of George Rogers Clark was properly a Virginia army rather than an American army, for Kentucky was then only a county of Virginia. The Northwest Territory had been considered a part of the enormous Virginia colony since the days of early settlement, and now the British had seized it with the aid of Indian tribes. To win approval of his daring invasion, and to get gunpowder and supplies, Clark had made the long journey east from Kentucky to the capital of Virginia at Williamsburg—more than two weeks on foot and horseback. Though he had lived on the frontier for years, Clark was returning home. He had been born on a farm adjoining Thomas Jefferson's Monticello, and Governor Patrick Henry had been his father's lawyer.

The young major in buckskins impressed Governor Henry and the leaders of his legislature. In the Assembly were Thomas Jefferson, George Mason, and Richard Henry Lee, wealthy planters who had led Virginia to rebellion. They promised the major and his men rewards in western lands if the attack on the Northwest succeeded. Governor Henry gave Clark secret orders to raise 350 men and offered £1200 in inflated Virginia currency to buy boats and ammunition at forts on the frontier. Most of the Virginia Assembly knew nothing of the plan, for Henry feared that word of the scheme might leak to the British. Clark was soon on his way west with money and gunpowder.

There was trouble at Fort Pitt, an outpost claimed by both Virginia and Pennsylvania, where officers quarreled with Clark over issuing supplies and mustering men for the expedition. Clark pleaded and threatened to no avail. These officials would give him no aid for a routine trip of exploration down the Ohio, and Clark could not tell them his true destination.

Fort Pitt was the only post within hundreds of miles where the major could get help. But he refused to give up, even when only a handful of men appeared to follow him, and even when some of these deserted rather than invade British territory. "It made me as desperate as I was before determined," Clark said. In that mood he set forth down the Ohio.

Within four days the boatmen were in enemy country. Clark's army met a party of hunters who had just come from Kaskaskia, and the major questioned them closely. Their report was encouraging. The enemy did not suspect an attack by an American force. Kaskaskia was held by Frenchmen who were now under British control. And the French feared Kentuckians—the "Long Knives" —more than they feared hostile Indians. Clark was pleased. He intended to play on the French fear of his frontiersmen before winning them over with kind treatment. The troops moved on, now confident of success. They soon had more good news.

William Linn, who had been left behind at the Falls of the Ohio, overtook them in his canoe after paddling alone through the wild country. He brought word that France had joined the United States in the war against England. This was just the news that Clark needed to win over the Frenchmen in Kaskaskia and Vincennes and turn them against their English masters.

Near the end of June, Clark beached his boats, hid them in the waterside thickets a few miles east of the junction of the Ohio and the Mississippi rivers, and began a march of 120 miles through deep woodlands to Kaskaskia. The men moved silently in single file, forbidden to build fires or to shoot their rifles at game. When food gave out after four days, the men lived on berries they picked along the trail. They were near starvation when they approached Kaskaskia on July 4 and saw the log fort across a small river. The enemy post gave no sign of alarm. The Kentuckians slept in hiding through the day, seized small boats along the river bank, and crossed the stream, leaving most of their clothing behind.

Clark and his chief lieutenant, Simon Kenton, led a party through the gate of the fort without challenge. They posted men throughout the sleeping village and then entered the cabin of the commander, Philippe Rastel, the Chevalier de Rocheblave, an officer now in British pay. The startled Frenchman awoke to see several half-naked Kentuckians standing over him. Grimy and unshaven, they looked quite as savage as the legendary reputations they had won in the wilderness. Rocheblave surrendered.

Outside, Clark's men shouted to arouse the people of the village.

French-speaking Kentuckians called orders: everyone must stay indoors or be shot. The village was in American hands. There were a few shrieks, and then Kaskaskia fell quiet. Clark wrote: "I don't suppose a greater silence ever Reagned among the Inhabitants of a place." Under Clark's orders his men moved about noisily all night searching houses for arms and food, deliberately frightening the people. In order to increase their fear, Clark told the Frenchmen nothing of his plans or his reason for the attack. Every trail into the fort was guarded and the village was cut off from the world so completely that it was to be a month before Henry Hamilton, in Detroit, learned of the capture.

The next morning Clark put a few of Rocheblave's troops in irons. Clark, outnumbered and deep in enemy territory, realized that he must impress the Kaskaskians. His opportunity came when a priest, Father Pierre Gibault, led a few men into Clark's headquarters cabin, obviously afraid of the Kentuckians. The priest asked if he could hold a meeting in the church, and Clark casually gave his permission. When the priest begged to have some of the villagers' clothing returned, Clark said, "Do you think Americans are savages, that we intend to strip women and children? My only aim is to bring peace to the Illinois country. And since France has now joined us in the war against England, you are free to join either side."

The French were shaken by this news, for they had known nothing of the French-American alliance. Within two days Clark had made fast friends of the Kaskaskians. He sent a company to seize the nearby outpost, Cahokia. The astonished French villagers of that place, who had been living under British military rule, were offered American citizenship and a free election for a magistrate. They cheerfully accepted Clark's proposal.

The major then tried to win over from British allegiance the Indian chiefs of the region. The chiefs were alarmed by Clark's bold raid and puzzled to see that their French allies were now at peace with the Kentuckians. Messengers were sent into the wilderness, and hundreds of Indians came to Clark's peace parley at Kaskaskia in late August, some of them from as far as five hundred miles away. The major handled them with skill, though he confessed that he was "under some apprehension among such a lot of devils." The chiefs had never heard such an orator as Clark. He offered no gifts and spoke no flattery. He warned the chiefs bluntly that they must desert the British and halt their raids on the Kentucky settlements—or the Long Knives would wipe them out. He gave the Indians his own version of the American Revolution:

> The Big Knives are very much like the Red People; they don't know well how to make blankets, powder and cloth. . . . They buy from the English [who] would not let our women spin, nor the men make powder, nor let us trade with anybody else. . . .
> At last the Great Spirit took pity on us and kindled a great council fire that never gave out, at a place called Philadelphia. . . . The old men . . . took up the hatchet, sharpened it and put it into [the] hands of the young men and told [them] to strike the English as long as they could find one on this side of the Great Water. . . . The English were driven from one place to another until they got weak and hired you Red People to fight for them. . . . The Great Spirit, getting angry at this, he caused your old Father and the French King and other nations to join the Big Knives and fight with them. . . .

Clark was astonished by the effect of his speech, which "did more service than a Regiment of Men could have done." Though he made no formal treaty, he agreed on peace with ten or twelve tribes and took them out of the war. He called on the Spanish governor, who controlled the region west of the Mississippi, and opened friendly relations. He sent Rocheblave as a prisoner to Williamsburg.

Then Clark planned his next assault, across the flooded Wabash country to Vincennes, which Colonel Hamilton had just occupied with a small force of militia and Indians. The Englishman was

George Rogers Clark, only 26 years old when his bold campaign se-
cured the entire Northwest Territory, sat for his portrait in later years.

confident that high waters caused by winter floods would make him
secure against attack. The stage was set for Clark's most dramatic
venture. The major wrote to Governor Henry:

> I am resolved to . . . risk the whole on a single battle . . . on
> this forlorn hope. I know the case is desperate, but Sir, we must
> either quit the country or attack Hamilton. . . . Great things have
> been effected by a few men well conducted. . . . In case we fail,
> though . . . this country as well as Kentucky, I believe, is lost.

Vincennes lay 240 miles away, over flooded prairies that had become a chain of lakes and ponds. It was February 7, 1779, when Clark and his men began their march through the cold waters and half-frozen mud. "I would have bound myself for seven years a slave to have had five hundred troops," Clark said. But he now had 127 men, 60 of them French volunteers.

Many of the men were mounted at first, but the water became so deep that horses could go no farther. The troops slogged on through the flooded Wabash bottomlands, often wading waist-deep for hours at a time. Still, they marched 174 miles in six days, until they reached the two branches of the Little Wabash, usually three miles apart but now joined in a huge lake. Clark's men built a boat and used it to find high ground many miles ahead and ferried themselves across the water. A drummer boy paddled himself over on his drum.

Clark tried constantly to bolster morale. At night, when they camped on soggy knolls rising from water, the men laughed and sang. "They really began to think themselves superior to other men," Clark said.

They floundered on through one morass after another under leaden skies. Rain fell almost every day. Sometimes the water was neck-deep on the tall Clark, who led the way, followed by shorter men who swam, hung to floating debris, or clung to each other as they struggled forward.

When their food was all gone, the men shot an occasional deer marooned by the flood and divided the carcass among the hungry marchers. They once found a fox crouched in a tree above the water, killed it, and roasted it over coals, eating even the intestines.

One day when the major saw that most of his troops were "alarmed and bewailing the situation," he led them onward by blacking his face with gunpowder, giving a war whoop and plunging into the water again. The column followed: "The party gazed and fell in, one after another, without saying a word, like a flock of sheep." He soon had them singing.

For several days they were so near Vincennes that they heard the morning gun of the fort at sunrise each day, but the way became so difficult and the men so weak that many wanted to give up and go no farther. Clark grimly posted riflemen in the rear to shoot down those who lagged, and the column cheered him.

When Clark had almost given up hope, they came upon some Indian squaws in a canoe loaded with buffalo meat, corn, tallow, and kettles. Buffalo soup made from these treasures gave the troops strength for the last few miles. As they came at last within sight of the log fort of Vincennes, Clark wrote of their relief: "Every man now feasted his eyes and forgot he had suffered anything."

On the night of February 23, Clark's men surrounded the fort, firing their rifles through cracks between its logs with deadly accuracy and shooting down gunners who opened ports to fire cannon. The besiegers moved about rapidly, laughing and talking in loud voices, to deceive Hamilton as to their numbers. There was brisk firing the next morning, during which one American was killed. After several hours of battle, Hamilton decided that resistance was useless. He sent out a white flag, asking for terms.

Clark demanded immediate surrender, saying that if he were forced to storm the palisade Hamilton could "depend upon such Treatment justly due to a Murderer." Hamilton gave up on terms little better than unconditional surrender. When Clark marched his two small and ragged companies into the fort to accept the British surrender, Hamilton stared in disbelief.

"Major Clark, where is your army?"

Clark waved to his thin ranks.

Hamilton turned away with tears in his eyes.

The garrison became prisoners of war, and Hamilton himself was sent to jail in Williamsburg, where he was to remain for almost three years.

The major returned the captured troops to Detroit, with a warning that the larger fort would be next. Clark never raided that outpost. Most of the great Northwest was now American territory, however. One by one the large Indian tribes, fearing loss of their lands and anxious to join the winning side, went to frontier forts and made peace with the Americans.

Thomas Jefferson, who became Virginia's governor in 1779, ordered Clark to build a fort at the forks of the Ohio to guard against British invasion. But the governor sent few men and no money. Clark was promoted to lieutenant colonel and the Virginia legislature awarded him a sword. That was little comfort to Clark. He had bought ammunition and supplies from frontier merchants for his daring expedition, pledging his own credit, and now Virginia would not pay the bills.

Once the Northwest was won, men seemed to forget Clark's brilliant exploits. Thomas Jefferson wrote George Washington of "the enterprizing and energetic genius of Clark." General Washington, who did not know the Kentuckian, wrote, "I do not think the charge of the enterprise could have been committed to better hands than Col. Clark's." But there was little more than praise for the conqueror of the frontier.

Virginia's legislature haggled over $20,000 in back pay due Clark for many years of service. The new state was near bankruptcy and could pay her soldiers only in land grants. When Clark was awarded land, creditors who had advanced supplies for his long marches seized it in settlement of his debts.

George Rogers Clark had fought only one campaign. But when peace negotiations came, his victory over Henry Hamilton at Vincennes allowed the Americans to claim a vast new territory. Under his fearless leadership a tiny band of brave men had helped to seize the upper Mississippi Valley for the United States. By his daring stroke Clark had added five future states to the Union— Indiana, Ohio, Illinois, Michigan, Wisconsin, and part of Minnesota. No troops of the Revolution had won victory against greater odds.

John Paul Jones

Victor at Sea

The moon rose from a cloud bank over the North Sea in the early darkness of September 23, 1779, and revealed two warships sailing along the English coast. From the towering chalk cliff of Flamborough Head a throng of Englishmen gazed out to sea, drawn by the promise of battle. It was a calm evening, the wind was light, and the sea was like glass.

One ship was the Royal Navy's *Serapis,* a new fifty-gun frigate commanded by Captain Richard Pearson. The other was a clumsy intruder, the forty-gun *Bonhomme Richard* of the upstart American Navy. The *Richard* was an old merchant ship converted to naval use by the French, a tired veteran of the tea trade sailed by a captain who called himself John Paul Jones. Most of her officers were American. But her decks swarmed with a crew picked up in France—Englishmen, Scots, Swedes, Portuguese, Norwegians, Swiss, and Italians, some of them lately from prisons. Clinging to her masts were some French marines, sharpshooters ready with their muskets.

The skipper was a slight, almost frail, figure of about five feet five inches, with a bold, defiant bearing. His face was thin and hollow-cheeked, with a sharp nose, hazel eyes, and a strong chin. He was thirty-two years old, with graying brown hair which was brushed firmly into a queue. He wore a fine new blue coat with white lapels, a ruffled neckcloth, and gilt epaulets on his shoulders. Even as he paced his deck he sipped frequently from a glass of limeade.

The two ships came closer and closer.

Captain Pearson bellowed across the water, "What ship is that?"

The *Richard* was edging nearer, flying a British flag to deceive the enemy. "The *Princess Royal!*" an officer yelled.

"Where from?"

There was no reply.

The *Serapis* hailed again: "Answer immediately or I will fire into you!"

The British colors dropped from the *Richard's* mast and a new American flag fluttered upward. The ships opened fire almost at the same instant. Two of the largest American guns burst, killing many of their crews and ripping out the deck overhead. The *Serapis* now had much greater firepower.

Onlookers ashore saw sulphur-yellow clouds shot with streaks of flame. The thunder of guns drew hundreds more to the cliffs. The ships turned in tight circles, seeking advantage. They drew within a hundred feet of each other. The big guns roared below decks, and muskets of sharpshooters popped in the rigging. The swifter *Serapis* raked the American's decks with shot.

To avoid this fire, Jones tried to board the enemy vessel. His one chance was to fight at close quarters. The English crew beat off the boarding party, but Jones tried once more, recklessly smashing the *Richard's* prow into the stern of the *Serapis*. Jones was now caught in an awkward position from which he could not train a single cannon on the enemy. The *Richard* seemed to be helpless.

John Paul Jones: A portrait bust based on the original sculpture by Houdon.

Captain Pearson called to ask if the American had surrendered. "Is your ship struck?"

Jones shouted from the quarterdeck, "I have not yet begun to fight!"

Jones maneuvered his sails. The ships pulled apart, still firing, jockeying for position, and soon they collided once more. The anchor of the *Serapis* hooked onto the *Richard,* and the ships were drawn together with their gun muzzles touching.

Jones yelled to his crew, "We've got her now! Throw the grappling irons! Stand by for boarding!"

He snatched a British line which had fallen across his deck and tied it firmly to a mast. One of his officers came to help him, cursing fiercely.

"Mr. Stacey, it's no time to be swearing," Jones said. "You may be in eternity in a moment."

There was chaos on the decks of both ships. British sailors who tried to throw off the grappling hooks fell under the musket fire and grenades of the French marksmen. Pearson dropped anchor, hoping that the wind and tide would swing the *Richard* free so that the *Serapis* could use her big guns. But the ships continued to turn, held tightly in their dance of death, the cannon still roaring. The sails of both ships caught fire.

For two hours the ships clung together, with casualties mounting, until the *Richard* had only three small guns left—nine-pounders on the quarterdeck, one of which Jones fired himself. By now the French marksmen had cleared the decks of the *Serapis*, where no man dared expose himself. But the British eighteen-pounders roared on from below, tearing the stout old *Richard* to

The guns of Flamborough Head: The battle between the Serapis *and the* Bonhomme Richard, *painted a few years later by a lieutenant of the Royal Navy.*

pieces. Jones's quarterdeck trembled upon a few remaining timbers, and only a miracle kept it from crashing into the gunroom below. But the *Richard*'s masts were steady, and sharpshooters still fired from the rigging.

There were other ships not far away—the *Vengeance, Pallas,* and *Alliance* of Jones's squadron and the British *Countess of Scarborough.* The *Pallas* cut the rigging of the *Countess of Scarborough* with so many shots that the British ship surrendered. Otherwise the badly wounded *Richard* and *Serapis* fought alone.

The sails of the American overhung the decks of the *Serapis,* so that Jones's men leapt into the enemy rigging, threw the Englishmen to the deck, and fired down into enemy hatches. One seaman dropped a grenade into a hatch and exploded gunpowder, killing at least twenty men and burning many others. Eight or ten fires raged on the *Serapis*.

Jones once became so exhausted that he sat on a chicken coop to rest.

A sailor begged him to lower the flag and surrender. "For God's sake, Captain," said the sailor, "strike!"

Jones leapt to his feet. "No! I may sink, but I'll never strike!" He began firing his nine-pounder once more.

Captain Pearson was on the point of giving up when the *Richard*'s chief gunner, Henry Gardner, shouted to Jones, begging that he ask the British for mercy: "Quarters, quarters! For God's sake!"

Jones pulled a pistol from his belt and flung it at Gardner's head, knocking him to the deck.

Pearson, who had heard the shout, called to Jones: "Sir, do you ask for quarter?"

"No, sir," Jones said, "I haven't thought of it. I'm determined to make you strike."

Pearson then shouted to his crew: "Boarders away!"

His men rushed toward the *Richard*'s deck—but were driven back by Jones's men, who waited with pikes and speared several Englishmen.

When the fight had raged until almost 10:30 P.M., a hundred prisoners, taken earlier from British ships, were freed from the *Richard*'s hold to man the pumps. One of these escaped to the *Serapis* and told Pearson to hold on for a few minutes, since the American was sinking. But the battered mainmast of the *Serapis* wavered dangerously, and Pearson gave up the fight. He had nailed the red British ensign to his mast. Now he tore it down with his own hands, since none of his men on deck could move.

The infant U.S. Navy had won its first significant victory at sea.

Jones went aboard the defeated *Serapis*. As he shook hands with Pearson, the British ship's mainmast crashed into the sea. Pearson gave his sword to Jones, who returned it, praising the gallant fight of the British. The captains then went into the wrecked cabin of the *Bonhomme Richard* for a glass of wine.

Jones and his survivors worked to save the old *Richard,* but she sank on the morning of September 25, and Jones moved his flag to the ruined *Serapis.* Each ship had lost more than 150 men.

It had been a small affair, as sea battles went, a hot fight of three hours and a half that had cost the powerful British Navy only two of its smaller ships. But the news astonished a world so long ruled by English sea power. The audacity of John Paul Jones, striking at the world's greatest navy in its home waters, gave new hope to the American rebels.

The victory was widely celebrated in France. Benjamin Franklin wrote to Jones that "scarce anything was talked of at Paris and Versailles but your cool Conduct and persevering Bravery during the terrible Conflict." Franklin had helped Jones to obtain the little French vessel—which was named *Bonhomme Richard* after the "Poor Richard" of Franklin's *Almanac.*

The original name of the gallant young captain was John Paul. He was the son of a gardener in Galloway, in southern Scotland. He spent his early years fishing and sailing in the great bay called Solway Firth, which lay before his home. Almost as soon as he could walk to the tiny nearby port of Carsethorn, John went down to climb over ships and to talk with sailors of their life at sea and in distant ports around the world. He and his playmates built small navies, and as John shouted commands the others maneuvered their rowboats as if in battle.

At the age of thirteen John became an apprentice to a local ship-owner. The boy agreed to sail and work for seven years for very little pay in order to learn the seaman's trade. He sailed with ships carrying slaves from Africa to America for a time, but was sickened by "the abominable trade" and left it in disgust. His master became bankrupt, and the young apprentice was free.

In 1768, when he was twenty-one, John got his first chance to prove himself. The master and mate of a small ship died of fever at sea, and John Paul, the only man aboard who could navigate, took command and steered her safely home. The owners made John her captain, and despite his youth he was off on a career as sailing master.

A captain's work was hard and endless, and his responsibility complete. He must give orders for handling sail, navigate by stars and sun, discipline the crew, stand a watch himself. When he reached a foreign port, he had to arrange the sale of his cargo and take aboard the most profitable cargo he could find for the return voyage. He must make all decisions himself, and skippers who made errors soon lost their ships. It was good training, and John learned quickly and well.

But young Captain Paul was not an easy man to sail with. He had a violent temper, and when his men did not carry out his orders to perfection, his wrath exploded. In 1770 John had his first serious trouble with a crewman, one Mungo Maxwell, a lazy, disobedient sailor who tried the captain's patience once too often. John had him tied in the rigging and flogged with a whip. Maxwell showed his scars to officers ashore and made a complaint against Captain Paul. A court dismissed the charge, but when Maxwell later died of fever, John Paul was imprisoned until he could prove his innocence. He was cleared of all blame in Maxwell's death.

Captain Paul was so well known in the shipping trade that he was soon made master and part owner of a large ship, the square-rigger *Betsey* of London, sailing between England and the West Indies.

By now, at twenty-six, John Paul was an expert ship handler, navigator, and trader, and was on his way to becoming wealthy when bad luck overtook him. His crew mutinied on the island of Tobago and chased John into his cabin. Captain Paul killed the leader of the mutiny with his sword, just as the sailor was about to strike him with a club. The captain went ashore to give himself up for trial, but friends convinced him that he could not get a fair trial on the island. John fled on another ship and sailed to America.

When he arrived on the mainland, or soon afterward, he had taken a new name—John Paul Jones. For many months he dropped out of sight, and little is known of his movements in those days. He visited a brother who lived in Virginia, and also spent some time in North Carolina.

In 1775, after the outbreak of the Revolution, Jones joined the new Continental Navy and became the first officer of his rank, a first lieutenant. He won his commission through a friend Joseph Hewes, a Congressman from North Carolina. Jones had made other friends among leaders of the Revolution, including Robert Morris of Pennsylvania and John Adams, the navy's great friend. Adams, overcoming the resistance of timid Congressmen, forced the building of the navy and urged promotion for its boldest captains, especially Jones.

Adams wrote about the extraordinary qualities in Jones:

> This is the most ambitious and intriguing officer in the American Navy. Jones has Art, and Secrecy, and aspires very high. Eccentricities and Irregularities are . . . in his Character, they are visible in his Eyes. His voice is soft and still and small, his eye has keenness and Wildness and softness in it.

It was a feeble little navy into which Jones went. The first four ships, all converted merchantmen, were commissioned in November 1775, a month before Jones became an officer. John went aboard one of them, the *Alfred,* commanded by Captain Dudley Saltonstall of Connecticut. Discipline was so bad that Jones and other officers had to stand the watch day and night to keep men from deserting.

The *Alfred* and other ships were sent to the West Indies to raid British islands, and they captured badly needed cannon and powder in the Bahamas. The little fleet of seven ships met no enemy

Jones was widely known for elegant clothes and a violent temper. This British drawing shows him shooting at a sailor who tried to give up the ship during a battle.

vessels until it neared home, when it fought and badly damaged
the British *Glasgow* near Block Island, off the Connecticut coast.
John Paul Jones commanded the *Alfred*'s gunners, who banged
away at the larger ship at close range during the hottest part of
the fight.

In May 1776, Jones became a captain. He commanded the sloop
Providence, with twelve guns and seventy-three men—the best
crew he ever commanded, the captain said later. He took the swift
little ship to sea alone. In forty-nine days he captured eight prize
ships, slipped away from two large British ships, and destroyed an
enemy fishing fleet off Nova Scotia.

Jones wrote frequent letters to his friends in Congress. He complained about his rank and about the navy's high command. And
he complained especially of the small prizes given to captains and
crews when enemy vessels were captured. British sailors were re-
warded much more handsomely. Congress soon offered a greater
share of booty for victors at sea—one-half of the value of each captured merchant ship, and the total value of a warship. The captains and crews of the navy shared in these prizes, and all became
eager to engage the enemy.

Jones returned to sea immediately, this time in command of the
Alfred, and took eight more prizes. One of them was a large ship
loaded with British uniforms, which Jones sent to General Washington's ragged army.

By now Congressmen considered Jones to be the boldest fighter
of the navy. John Hancock wrote to Robert Morris, "I admire the
spirited conduct of little Jones; pray push him out again. I know
he does not love to be idle." Jones was soon at sea once more, this
time with a new ship, the *Ranger,* built in Maine. She sailed to
France with news of the astonishing American victory at Saratoga,
and captured two rich prizes on the way. From France, Jones took
the *Ranger* into the home waters of the enemy to raid the coast—
the first hostile raid against England in more than a hundred years.
He conquered another British warship, the *Drake,* terrorized the

British people, maddened the Royal Navy, and won the only American victories in the darkest months of the Revolution.

John Paul Jones preached the doctrine of sea power as a strategic force. "Without a Respectable Navy," he said, "alas America!" He had done more than anyone else to make his country's tiny navy respectable. He also foresaw that America would build the greatest of all navies. "It will rise as if by Enchantment," he wrote, "and become . . . the wonder and Envy of the World."

During the Revolution, the United States was unable to build a navy to match the British. After France became an ally, French ships inevitably played the main part in the fighting at sea. Still, Jones was not forgotten. His skill and bravery lifted American morale in a time of defeat and despair. No one did more to build the traditions of the U.S. Navy than the Scottish gardener's boy who won victories as astounding to his friends as to his foes.

Few people could imagine how this young captain had caused such havoc at sea. Abigail, the wife of John Adams, was one who understood. She wrote after meeting Jones:

> I expected to have seen a rough, stout warlike Roman—instead of that I should sooner think of wrapping him up in cotton wool, and putting him in my pocket, than sending him to contend with cannon-balls. He is small of stature, well proportioned, soft in speech, easy in his address, polite in his manners. . . . Under all this appearance of softness he is bold, enterprising, ambitious and active.

Mrs. Adams would also have sensed the will power of this fierce little captain when he said, as he sought a flagship to carry the war to England: "I wish to have no Connection with any Ship that does not sail fast, for I intend to go in harm's way." This was his creed of life and became that of the United States Navy.

Nathanael Greene

Savior of the South

A freezing wind swept the Delaware River on Christmas night of 1776. Great blocks of ice swirled down the flooded stream, crashing against the hulls of boats at the crossing. On the Pennsylvania shore, soldiers wrapped in sodden rags struggled to load cannon and horses on the small craft. George Washington's army, despised and defeated, was moving to attack an enemy outpost at Trenton, New Jersey—its most daring move in a year and a half of war.

The Commander in Chief was at the riverside. Among his officers was a remarkable soldier, General Nathanael Greene from Rhode Island, who had been dismissed from his pacifist Quaker meeting when he joined the army. Tonight Greene was cheery and alert despite the icy wind and the dangers that lay ahead. The desperate attack on which the army risked its existence was largely his idea. He did not see well as he peered over the river, for one of the blue eyes in his round, ruddy face had been injured in his youth. As he moved among the men he also limped, from an earlier accident at his father's ironworking forge. The men liked

Greene, though they found him a bit odd. He often stopped on the hardest marches to brew a cup of tea and to read from books he carried in his pockets—books by ancient authors such as Plutarch and Julius Caesar, or by more modern military experts such as Sharp and Turenne.

Just before the troops crossed, officers read aloud the stirring words of Thomas Paine's *The Crisis,* which gave them new courage. But despite the urging of Greene and others the little army was late in reaching the New Jersey shore, and there were still nine miles to march. The weather grew worse before sunrise. Snow and sleet made the roads like glass. Washington and Greene could only hope that the hired German regiments holding Trenton for the British were still asleep. The little band of 2400 Americans divided and wound toward Trenton on separate roads.

Dawn had come before the first men reached the village and were discovered by a few wakeful Germans. Musket fire broke out and the alarm was given. Germans poured into the streets and began shooting, but it was too late. Henry Knox's cannon drove them back. Other startled Hessians, stumbling sleepily from their warm beds, came out to surrender to the ragged and shivering Americans who swarmed everywhere about the barracks. Within a few minutes the battle of Trenton was over—a startling victory which gave new hope to all Americans, their first real victory of the war.

The first men in Trenton on this chill morning were the troops of Nathanael Greene. As Washington's chief adviser, Greene had shared the blame for early American defeats. But after this day he was to become a hero, credited with the daring plan of attack which routed or captured the entire garrison of Trenton. Many officers thought Greene was the most able commander in the American armies.

Nathanael had been barely out of infancy when his father set him to hard work at the family forge in Coventry, Rhode Island.

The boy grew strong from years of labor. A tutor drilled him in reading, writing, and arithmetic for a few months. But the tutor was dismissed by Nathanael's father, who thought further education too sinful and worldly for his sons. So the boy had to educate himself. He was near manhood before his father realized that Nathanael's stolen knowledge of books was a good influence. Greene found an unusual bookshop in Boston owned by Henry Knox. Here a wider world of knowledge was opened to Nathanael. He gathered a library of two hundred volumes, bartering for his books with toy anchors he made at the forge. He kept a copy of Euclid by the forge until he mastered geometry. Greene read history, bookkeeping, science, and law, and for a few months practiced law in his home town.

As tension grew between the American colonists and the British occupation troops, Nathanael began to drill with a local militia company. At the opening of the war young Greene, now in charge of the family business, converted his ironworks into a cannon factory. After the fighting at Lexington and Concord, when troops were being mustered in all the colonies, Greene was named brigadier general and put in command of Rhode Island troops. He took his regiments to Boston, where the British were besieged, and Rhode Island's well-equipped soldiers were soon known as among the army's finest. Greene's precise rows of tents stood out amid the scattering of hovels thrown up by other New England troops. When George Washington arrived to take command, he saw that Greene was a dependable leader. The Rhode Islander rose rapidly in the regular army.

When the British were driven from Boston and moved against New York, Greene was chosen to command the key position on Long Island and built earthworks there. Though the army met one defeat after another, Greene's leadership was recognized. He was promoted to corps commander, in charge of several divisions of the army, and became more important as the war wore on. He helped to choose the ground for defense for the battle of Brandy-

Nathanael Greene and George Washington at the battle of Trenton (following the Delaware crossing shown on page 57). This was painted by George Washington Parke Custis, adopted son of the Commander in Chief.

wine, near Philadelphia. And he led large bodies of troops at the battles of Germantown and Monmouth.

During the bitter winter at Valley Forge, when the army was near starvation, Washington made Greene his Quartermaster General. Conditions improved rapidly, though Greene could not entirely overcome the shortages which had plagued the army for so long.

One of Washington's most trusted officers, the dashing Benedict Arnold, shocked the country by attempting to sell possession of the fort at West Point, New York, for British gold. Alert American sentries captured Major John André, a British agent, who had conspired with Arnold, but the traitor himself escaped into British lines. Washington ordered a trial for Major André. As president of this all-important court martial, Washington named Nathanael

Greene. The court found André guilty and ordered him hanged.

In 1780 after the tide of war rolled southward, and the British threatened to defeat the colonies one by one, Washington sent the Rhode Islander to his most difficult task. The redcoats seemed invincible in the South, and if Greene could not stop them, the American cause was lost.

In two years of savage fighting in the South, the British had conquered South Carolina and Georgia. Those colonies were already suffering from years of bitter civil war, in which patriot and Tory neighbors looted and burned each other's homes and often killed their former friends from ambush. After storming Charleston and capturing an entire American army, the redcoats had swept into upland South Carolina, where Lord Cornwallis routed a large force under General Horatio Gates at the battle of

Camden. The South lay helpless before the invaders. Only a few guerrilla bands defied the redcoats.

A string of British forts now dominated the interior. North Carolina was open to conquest, and the road to Virginia would soon be open. When Washington sent Greene to save the South, it seemed almost too late. The Commander in Chief wrote Congress glumly: "I think I am giving you a General; but what can a General do without men, without arms, without clothing, without stores, without provisions?"

Congress had no help for Greene. So he rode southward, almost alone, begging state governors for men, guns, wagons, horses, food, ammunition. There was little to be had. "They all promised fair," he wrote, "but I fear will do little."

While Greene was on his way south he was cheered by news of an astonishing victory at King's Mountain, South Carolina. There a band of mountain men had destroyed an army of Tories, killing or wounding most of the band and leading others away as prisoners. Along the South Carolina coast, in the lowland swamps, the guerrilla leader Francis Marion stung the British with sneak attacks, sniping at stragglers, seizing outposts, striking by night. The redcoats hunted Marion for months, without so much as a glimpse of him.

Lord Cornwallis was now becoming uneasy over the hit-and-run warfare of the border country. He complained to his superior, Sir Henry Clinton, about American tactics:

> They always keep at a considerable distance, and retire on our approach. The perpetual risings in different parts of this province . . . keep the whole country in continual alarm, and render the assistance of regular troops everywhere necessary.

The arrival of Greene made the earl even more uneasy.

The former Quaker reached Charlotte, North Carolina, in December 1780. He found eight hundred ragged men, the remnant

OHIO R.

KANAWHA R.

CUMBERLAND R.

CLINCH R.

HOLSTON R.

VOLICHUCKY R.

YADKIN R.

POTOMAC R.

MARYLAND

CHESAPEAKE BAY

• Charlottesville
Hanover C.H.

JAMES R.

Richmond

VIRGINIA

Williamsburg
Gloucester
Yorktown

Petersburg •

Jamestown

Portsmouth • Norfolk

DAN R.

ROANOKE R.

Halifax •

Hillsborough •

NORTH
CAROLINA

Guilford C.H. •

Salisbury •

King's Mountain ⚔ • Charlotte

Cowpens ⚔

Winnsboro •

Cheraw •
⚔ Hobkirk's
Hill

Camden •

NEUSE R.

New Bern •

CAPE FEAR R.

PEEDEE R.

⚔ Moore's Creek Bridge

Wilmington •

WATEREE R.

SALUDA R.

Ninety-
Six ⚔

Kettle
Creek ⚔

Augusta •

SOUTH
CAROLINA

SANTEE R.

Georgetown •

Eutaw ⚔
Springs

• Monck's Corner

COOPER R.

SANTEE R.

SULLIVAN'S ISLAND

BRIAR CREEK

Beaufort •

Charleston

OGEECHEE R.

SAVANNAH R.

GEORGIA

Port Royal •

Savannah •
Sunbury •

TYBEE
ISLAND

ALTAMAHA R.

SATILLA R.

ST. MARYS R.

St. Augustine •

GULF OF

MEXICO

EAST

FLORIDA

N

ATLANTIC

OCEAN

The
WAR in the SOUTH

0   Miles   200

palacios

of an army, with only three days' rations in camp. He wrote to officer friends:

> A few ragged, half starving troops in the wilderness, destitute of everything. . . . The country is almost laid waste and the inhabitants plunder one another with little less than savage fury. We live from hand to mouth. . . . More than half our numbers are in a manner naked, so much so that we cannot put them on the least kind of duty. Indeed there is a great number that have not a rag of clothes on them except a little piece of blanket in the Indian form around their waist.

Greene began at once to transform the hapless band into an army. His couriers galloped through the Carolinas in all directions, carrying orders. Engineers gathered boats on swift North Carolina rivers, ready for use in case of retreat. Officers rode through the country, begging or seizing farm horses. A prison camp was built in the rear of the army. Lead was sent from a mine in western Virginia to make musket balls. Women in Salisbury, North Carolina, made denim overalls and shirts. Country blacksmiths made horseshoes. Foragers gathered food. Powder magazines were set up in the interior. Salt boiled from sea water was hauled in from the coast.

General Washington sent a thousand muskets and half a dozen cannon from the North. Best of all, Lieutenant Colonel "Light-Horse" Harry Lee arrived with three hundred Virginia cavalrymen to join a small force under a kinsman of the Commander in Chief, Major William Washington. Within a few weeks, as Colonel Lee said, Greene had "infused a spirit of exalted patriotism" in his men and won their hearts. Reinforcements now came into camp—volunteers, recruits, and even criminals, sentenced to serve in the army rather than go to prison.

Greene rebuilt his army with the aid of an able staff, including Harry Lee and William Washington, who led Virginia dragoons mounted on fine plantation horses. Another aide was Brigadier General Daniel Morgan, an old Indian fighter and a veteran of Northern campaigns who came out of retirement.

Greene's first move was so bold that even the frontier fighter Morgan was surprised. The general divided his tiny force. He sent Morgan westward with about six hundred men, to pick up other troops on his way, under orders to worry the enemy but not to risk everything in a pitched battle. Cornwallis rose to the bait, sending his cavalry chief, Colonel Banastre Tarleton, after Morgan with a thousand crack troops and two cannon. The British colonel, who was accustomed to driving poorly trained Carolina militiamen before him, took up the chase with great confidence. He found Morgan more quickly than he expected.

Daniel Morgan, his army now almost as strong as Tarleton's, chose a battleground on an open hillside in western South Carolina. It was the site of an old pasture on a cattle trail, a place known as "The Cowpens." Morgan posted his men there and waited. Many of his officers thought that Morgan was foolhardy to confront redcoat veterans in such a place. But Morgan knew his troops, many of them squirrel hunters and Indian fighters who, though untrained in formal battle, were among the best marksmen in the world. He placed riflemen in the woods behind to shoot down any man who fled, and waited for Tarleton's troops.

They came in the chilly dawn of January 17, 1781.

Fifty of the enemy cavalry charged, expecting to drive the American rabble as usual. But the backwoods riflemen emptied fifteen British saddles. Tarleton's infantry moved up the slope, walking slowly and pausing now and then to fire volleys. Again the American rifles took a deadly toll. Many British officers fell. The American front lines were ordered to retire after a few rounds.

A British voice raised a shout, "They're running! Charge 'em!"

The redcoats broke ranks and dashed recklessly up the hill. Morgan's cavalry struck them in the flank and his infantry, which had fallen back in good order, turned and poured fire into the dis-

Cavalry charge at the battle of Cowpens.

"The Battle of Cowpens" by Frederick Kemmelmeyer from the Yale University Art Gallery, Mabel Brady Garven Collection

organized British. Within a few minutes Tarleton's force was destroyed. British losses were about 100 dead, 229 wounded, and 600 prisoners. Only a handful escaped with Tarleton to return to Cornwallis and the main army.

Morgan's losses were only 12 killed and 60 wounded. But he retreated immediately, herding his prisoners northward in an effort to escape Cornwallis. The earl plunged after him but was slowed by hundreds of Negro slaves who had fled their masters and flocked after the British, consuming army food and looting and burning the countryside. Cornwallis had begun a chase that would take him hundreds of miles through hostile country, dangerously far from his base. He burned most of his wagons to increase the army's speed, but could not overtake the Americans.

When he got news of the astounding victory of Cowpens, Greene joined Morgan and led the combined army northward, hurrying from river to river to escape the enemy. At the Yadkin River near Salisbury, North Carolina, he escaped Cornwallis by only a few hours. Gathering all boats and scows on the north bank to prevent pursuit, he forced Cornwallis to make a long detour upstream to find a shallow crossing. Greene had gained several days on the enemy.

Both armies suffered in the wintry weather. Greene wrote Washington:

> The miserable situation of the troops for want of clothing has rendered the march the most painful imaginable, with hundreds tracking the ground with bloody feet. Myself and my aides are almost worn out with fatigue. . . . The army is in good spirits notwithstanding its suffering and excessive fatigue.

Washington understood the purpose of Greene's campaign. "Your retreat before Cornwallis," he wrote, "is highly applauded by all ranks, and reflects much honor on your military abilities."

Greene retreated across the Dan River into Virginia, once more crossing just as British cavalry appeared on the south bank. Cornwallis turned back. Greene went into camp and begged Governor Thomas Jefferson for men and supplies.

Jefferson on another occasion complained of the army's seizure of horses from Virginia.

Greene replied angrily, "Are your horses dearer than your liberty?"

When Greene's appeals were heard at last and his army had grown to 4200 men, he returned to North Carolina and took a position at a country crossroads called Guilford Courthouse.

The armies met here on March 15. For two hours or more they clashed in one of the most savage battles of the Revolution. Greene's untrained North Carolina militia fled after firing one volley. But mountaineer riflemen on their flanks continued to fire, and many redcoats fell. The British next charged a line of Virginians who lay in a dense woodland. There the fight was long and bloody, with heavy casualties on both sides. The Virginians held for half an hour and then fled in disorder.

The battles came to a climax in a small meadow where the Maryland and Delaware regulars waited with two cannon. Men fought hand to hand. The American cannon were lost in a charge and retaken in a countercharge. At last the soldiers fought with stones, fists, and musket butts. When the aroused Americans pushed the redcoats backward, Cornwallis, with ruthless desperation, fired into the mingled mass with grapeshot from his cannon. The hail of lead drove the rebels from the field but also killed and wounded some of his own men.

When night fell the Americans retreated to a nearby mill and Cornwallis held the field—but he had lost 600 men killed and wounded, more than a quarter of his force. Aside from the runaway militia, who could be reassembled, Greene had lost only 150 men. The British retreated toward the sea at Wilmington, North Carolina. Their attempt to destroy Greene had been a costly failure.

Greene was more determined than ever. "We fight, get beat, rise, and fight again," he wrote. "We bear beating very well, and . . . the more we are beat, the better we grow."

Although Cornwallis claimed a victory at Guilford Courthouse, the campaign had badly weakened his army. Sir Henry Clinton, the British commander in America, wrote from New York, "His Lordship has lost an army, lost the object for which he moved it, and buried himself on the seacoast of North Carolina." And when news of the battle reached London, the Whig leader Charles Fox said, "Another such victory would ruin the British Army."

When he saw that Cornwallis had left South Carolina open to reconquest, Greene marched south against the few British forces remaining there. In a series of brisk little battles he drove the enemy from upland South Carolina. By the time Cornwallis had moved up the coast to Yorktown, Virginia, Greene had regained almost the entire South for the rebel cause.

After the war Greene fell into debt, like many other officers who served throughout the Revolution. Despite grants of land in South Carolina and Georgia, he did not prosper. He died in 1786, just three years after the signing of the peace treaty with England, and was buried in Savannah, Georgia.

He was praised by a fellow officer as "the greatest military genius" of the Revolution, and by Thomas Jefferson as "second to no one in enterprise, in resource, in sound judgment, promptitude of decision, and every other military talent." Jefferson never forgot Greene's angry impatience when he was refused Virginia horses for his army. But the author of the Declaration of Independence knew well that Greene had saved the South and in doing so had made victory possible.

George Washington

Commander in Chief

Soldiers had built a small pavilion on the east bank of the Hudson. General Washington sat there, shaded from the burning sun by a roof of leafy branches, watching the French troops cross to Haverstraw in a rickety fleet of scows and barges. At his side was Comte de Rochambeau, commander of the newcomers. The troops were splendid in white linen with pastel silk lapels, some of the oldest and proudest of French regiments. The sergeants wore ostrich plumes in their hats. The cavalrymen, many of them hired Polish troops, wore tall fur hats and scarlet pants and sat on saddle cloths of tiger skin. Washington watched them intently.

It was August 1781. The reserved general from Virginia could hardly conceal his elation at the arrival of his French allies after six years of lonely struggle. Only four months earlier he had been in despair:

> We are at this hour approaching fast to nakedness. Our hospitals are without medicines and our Sick without Nutriment. . . .

We are at the end of our tether, and now or never our deliverance must come.

Today he watched five thousand of the troops who had come to help save the revolutionary cause. Without these disciplined foreign veterans, Washington knew, the war could never be won.

His own army had already crossed, a small and tattered force, but fighters all the same. Of them another French count had recently said:

> I cannot insist too strongly how I was surprised by the American army. It is truly incredible that troops almost naked, poorly paid, and composed of old men and children and Negroes should behave so well on the march and under fire.

Negroes had fought in American ranks throughout the war, and on this march two-thirds of the crack Rhode Island regiment were blacks who had won French praise for their marching and discipline. One of the first to die in the rebel cause had been Crispus Attucks, a Negro killed in the Boston Massacre. Since then hundreds of slaves had won their freedom by fighting in Washington's army.

The long war had aged Washington. His strong face was lined, the queue of hair on his neck was streaked with gray, and his mouth had lost some of its firmness because of missing teeth.

The French found him dignified and imposing. One of Rochambeau's officers said of Washington, "I have never seen anyone who was more naturally and spontaneously polite. . . . He asks few questions, listens attentively, and answers in low tones and with few words." Another Frenchman wrote that Washington had no single striking feature, and that one left him with a vague memory of "a fine man . . . a fine figure, an exterior plain and modest . . . a manly courage, an uncommon capacity for grasping the whole scope of a subject."

The French thought the general amazing in other ways. For all his sternness, Washington was sometimes boylike, as when he played ball with his officers in camp, running and throwing for hours.

Count Axel Fersen, a Swedish soldier who came with the French, saw something else in the commander: "A tinge of melancholy affects his whole being, which is not unbecoming; it renders him more interesting."

When Washington rose from his seat and went down to a boat, the French troops could see that he was much larger than he had seemed when seated. He was well over six feet tall, spare and muscular, weighing more than two hundred pounds. Although he was almost fifty years old, he walked with the light step of a much younger man. The general had ridden horses and hunted foxes in Virginia almost as long as he could remember. He was an impressive but not a handsome man. His head seemed too small for his body, and his strong face, like those of many people of his day, bore the scars of smallpox.

Washington crossed the river to his headquarters in a farmhouse to plan the moves of the allied army from New York State down the long roads to Virginia. Few men in his armies knew where they were bound, but they gossiped in camp as all soldiers do. British spies who swarmed through the camp took these rumors to Sir Henry Clinton in New York City, warning that the allies were on their way to Virginia. Clinton, an intelligent but overcautious general, made no move to stop them. He feared an attack on New York itself, and was not yet sure where the French and Americans were heading.

Washington's own troops watched him carefully for a hint of what lay ahead, but even his officers watched from a distance. He did not encourage affection. Only one man was known to have called the general George, and he drew only an icy stare. Yet his wife called him "my old man," and some of the frontier troops called him "Old Hoss."

Soldiers told endless stories about him. They claimed that he was the strongest man in the armies. They said that he rarely lost his temper or swore in anger but that, when he did, wise men stayed out of his sight. Washington kept a stern discipline. Several times during the war he hanged deserters by the roadside without a trial, in order to discourage other soldiers from running away.

It was now more than six years since the day in Philadelphia when John Adams had proposed Washington as Commander in Chief. The wisdom and foresight of Adams, in choosing Washington, had been vital to the American cause. At times it seemed that it was Washington, almost alone, who had kept the Revolution alive. His iron will to win had been worth many regiments of soldiers. Through defeats and shortages, mutinies, betrayals and treason, the ruin of the currency, wholesale desertions by hungry, half-naked troops—it was always George Washington who refused to give up. It was Washington who kept alive a spirit of resistance among his small band of devoted officers and men.

He was not a foolish optimist. On the day he took control of the army he told Congress, "I do not think myself equal to the command I am honoured with." A few hours later he said to Patrick Henry, his fellow Virginian, "Remember, Mr. Henry, what I now tell you: From the day I enter upon the command of the American armies, I date my fall, and the ruin of my reputation."

Washington was among the first to speak of war against Great Britain. In 1769, six years before the outbreak of fighting, he urged a boycott of British goods to protest laws restricting American commerce:

> At a time when our lordly Masters in Great Britain will be satisfied with nothing less than the deprication of American freedom . . . no man shou'd scruple, or hesitate a moment to use arms in defence of so valuable a blessing.

Soon after the Boston Tea Party and the British closing of the

George Washington, shown by the artist Charles Willson Peale with cannon, horse, and flags.

port of Boston, Washington decided that it was too late for further petitions to London:

> Shall we . . . whine and cry for relief, when we have already tried it in vain? Or shall we supinely sit and see one province after another fall a prey to despotism? . . . I think the Parliament of Great Britain hath no more right to put their hands into my pocket, without my consent, than I have to put my hands into yours for money.

Shortly after Washington became Commander in Chief, he inspected the New England troops outside Boston. He found them "the most indifferent people I ever saw . . . exceedingly dirty and nasty people." But he predicted that they would fight well under proper leadership. And he found some of his most devoted and able officers in New England—men like Nathanael Greene and Henry Knox.

By the end of the year Washington was disgusted with the coming and going of militiamen who signed for a few months in the ranks and refused to serve longer despite the plight of their country. At moments even he seemed to despair of America's future:

> Such a dearth of public spirit, and want of virtue I never saw before, and pray God I may never be witness to again. . . . I tremble at the prospect. . . . Could I have foreseen what I have, and am likely to experience, no consideration upon earth should have induced me to accept this command.

Yet Washington's determination did not fail. In the spring of 1776, after General Knox dragged cannon over snowy roads from Fort Ticonderoga, the British evacuated Boston. Washington led his troops triumphantly into the city, which was to remain in American hands until the end of the war.

When the tide of battle turned southward from Boston, the new

Commander in Chief discovered that he had much to learn. Thirty-two thousand British troops landed near New York, and Washington's men were defeated in savage battles on Long Island, at Brooklyn, Harlem Heights, and White Plains. He also lost Fort Washington, an important post on the Hudson.

The general and his army had failed their first great test. The half-trained and ill-equipped troops had often run from the bayonets of the redcoats and their hired German regiments. Washington shared the blame since his plan of battle permitted the enemy to outflank his line and come into his rear. These hard lessons taught him caution in combat. His lifelong habit of patience hardened into a fierce doggedness.

Though his troops continued to run away from battle and to desert in droves, though he was always short of money, arms, and ammunition, the Virginian kept up the struggle. After the terrible defeats around New York his troops fell back through New Jersey, apparently beaten. But their victory at Trenton at Christmastime of 1776 gave Americans new hope.

Somehow the army endured through the pitched battles near Philadelphia. When it emerged from the terrible winter at Valley Forge, thanks in large part to Baron von Steuben, it was tougher and better trained. The troops soon met the redcoats again at Monmouth Courthouse, and though victory escaped them they fought bravely and well. This was Washington's last major battle in the North.

Through three years of stalemate, Sir Henry Clinton barricaded himself in New York City. Washington waited outside, threatening to attack. Meanwhile, the war moved into the Southern colonies, where Nathanael Greene, Daniel Morgan, and Lafayette led American forces against Lord Cornwallis.

Washington, who was self-educated as a military man, had learned many lessons. Early in the war he gave up reading European books on strategy. Instead he consulted with his younger associates, who also lacked formal military training but were brilliant and original in thought. They included Benedict Arnold, who was the war's greatest combat leader until he turned traitor; the former Boston bookseller, huge Henry Knox; Nathanael Greene; and still younger men like Lafayette, Alexander Hamilton, and John Laurens. Washington promoted these officers, followed their advice, and profited from experience. Gradually, he assumed complete control of the army. Though his methods caused bickering in Congress, and critics said that Washington sought to become a dictator, his policies made victory possible in the end.

In the summer of 1781, Washington and his newly arrived French ally, Rochambeau, saw their great opportunity. Now the victory which had so long eluded the rebels might be won.

British forces in America were divided. Sir Henry Clinton occupied New York City, Lord Cornwallis was holed up in Yorktown, and another redcoat force occupied Charleston. After the French army landed at Newport, Rhode Island, and marched down to join him, Washington had two choices. He could attack New York. Or, if the city's defenses were too strong, as Rochambeau argued, there was an even more exciting prospect in Virginia. If the young Marquis de Lafayette held Cornwallis in place, and a French fleet sailed into Chesapeake Bay to hold off the British Navy, an entire redcoat army might be trapped. Perhaps Great Britain would give up the struggle.

And so it was that in August the French and the Americans met at the Hudson River for the march southward. They hoped that a powerful French fleet under Admiral de Grasse would arrive to blockade Cornwallis from the sea.

Washington's troops built ovens on the New Jersey shore within sight of British lines, as if the French and Americans meant to spend the winter there. American gun crews carried cannon to the beach near Sandy Hook, and marched as if they planned to attack Staten Island. British officers in New York peered at all this activity through field glasses. Sir Henry Clinton built new forts, tore

Alexander Hamilton, a portrait by the Revolutionary artist John Trumbull. Both men served on General Washington's military staff, Hamilton from the age of 20 and Trumbull from the age of 19.

down houses to give his cannon clear fields of fire—and called on Lord Cornwallis to send more troops from Yorktown to help defend New York.

Even now, as Washington and Rochambeau crossed the Hudson and marched down through New Jersey, they did so in great secrecy. They refused to tell their officers and men where the next day's march would lead. Only when bugles blew reveille at 3 A.M. each morning did the army learn its route for the day.

In New York, Clinton got a flurry of reports from his spies. The French and Americans were on the move southward, said the spies. Day after day Clinton read these reports, looked across the river at his enemies—and did nothing to halt their movement. The British general gave signs of great nervous tension. He hid himself

French cannon may still be seen at Yorktown.

for three or four days at a time, refusing to see anyone. He complained of attacks of temporary blindness. He delayed making a decision until it was too late. By the end of August, the French and Americans had disappeared to the south. Only then did Clinton send a warning to Cornwallis that Washington was on the way.

Clinton was not entirely to blame for British troubles. Cornwallis marched to Virginia without orders in a move quite contrary to Clinton's intentions. But Clinton was anxious to return to England and have Cornwallis succeed him in command, and so he did not give the earl firm orders.

The people of Philadelphia cheered as the allied armies marched through the city on their way to Virginia. But many bystanders were shocked to see the contrast between the lean, ragged Americans and the beautifully dressed French. Washington's troops threatened mutiny in the city. They had not been paid for months, and some of them had not been paid during the war. The commander also had bad news from his scouts who watched New York: A British fleet had sailed for the south. Perhaps it would reach Chesapeake Bay in time to rescue Cornwallis. And still there was no news from Admiral de Grasse and the French fleet.

So the long march might be in vain. But Washington pushed the troops forward.

In Chester, Pennsylvania, a few miles south of Philadelphia, a dusty rider on a hard-breathing horse brought a dispatch which Washington tore open and read eagerly: Admiral de Grasse was in Chesapeake Bay! For once in his life Washington forgot himself. For a moment he was no longer the dignified Commander in Chief. He danced like a schoolboy before his gaping aides, waved a handkerchief, twirled his hat above his head, and ran to embrace Rochambeau, shouting the good news. If De Grasse could hold off the British fleet, and if Cornwallis remained in Yorktown, the allied armies had only to reach Virginia and surround the fortified village.

The general paid his troops in gold and silver coins borrowed

from the French, and the allies hurried southward in high spirits. There was no further talk of mutiny.

Washington rode ahead of them so swiftly that officers could hardly keep pace. In one day he rode sixty hard miles to reach Mount Vernon, which he had not seen since the beginning of the war. His family and servants were dismayed to see how six years of terrible responsibility had aged him.

By the middle of September, three weeks after leaving the Hudson, he was in Williamsburg. He was greeted happily by Lafayette, who hugged him and, as one officer said, "kissed him from ear to ear." The next day Washington had the most welcome news of

General Charles O'Hara, second in command to Lord Cornwallis, surrendered his sword after the British defeat at Yorktown. The French and American officers shown around George Washington included Rochambeau, Hamilton, Knox, and Lafayette.

all—De Grasse had defeated and driven off the British fleet! In a sharp battle of three hours, the French had set fire to several English ships, killing and wounding many men. The French losses were light. After drifting for a few days within sight of each other the fleets drew apart, and the British ships returned to New York for repairs.

Two weeks later, when all their men and guns had arrived from the North, Washington, Rochambeau, and Lafayette marched their combined army of 15,000 the few miles from Williamsburg to Yorktown. There they surrounded Cornwallis' army of 7500.

At first the allied troops dug trenches by day and night, pushing ever nearer to the besieged redcoats, who blazed away at them defiantly. Baron von Steuben, the American army's Inspector General, took his turn as commander of troops in the front lines. Hundreds of men tugged at ropes to drag artillery into position, until at last the allied artillery was ready to open fire on Yorktown. Somehow, Henry Knox had assembled enough heavy cannon and ammunition to make his gunners as effective as the well-trained French.

Washington himself fired the first shot from an American battery, a huge iron ball which ricocheted among the houses of the village. For eight days a terrible barrage of shells fell upon Yorktown, blasting houses, killing and maiming hundreds of soldiers and civilians, and driving Cornwallis into a cave in the bluff on the river bank. The sandy peninsula shook with the endless roar of the cannonade. Finally, on October 17, a redcoat drummer boy climbed to the top of a parapet and beat his drum furiously in the midst of the firing. It was a call for an armistice.

British and American officers met the next day to arrange terms of surrender. On October 19 the British and German soldiers filed out of Yorktown and gave up their weapons. On that very day, after many delays, Sir Henry Clinton sailed from New York with a fleet to relieve Cornwallis—too late. Washington allowed Cornwallis and most of his officers to return to England, but more than seven thousand redcoats were marched off to American prisons. Washington sent a courier to Philadelphia with news of victory. There were wild celebrations in every city and village as word spread through the country.

Washington feared that the victory at Yorktown would cause Americans to relax and give up their struggle for freedom. But as the months passed it became clear that the battles of the Revolution were over. A peace treaty was signed two years later and the new American nation was safely established.

In December 1783, Washington said his farewells in New York, where the British occupation forces were leaving for home. At

On Evacuation Day, British troops rowed from New York to the ships waiting to take them home. To delay replacement of their flag, they had greased the flagpole. But David von Arnsdale, a young American sailor, managed to scramble up and fly the new American flag.

Fraunces Tavern he said goodby to his officers in a simple, touching ceremony. Washington held up a glass of wine and said in a
choking voice, "With a heart full of love and gratitude, I now take
leave of you. I most devoutly wish that your later days may be as
prosperous and happy as your former ones have been glorious and
honorable."

When all the officers in the crowded room had drunk to the
toast, Washington was in tears. He said, "I cannot come to each
of you but shall feel obliged if each of you will come and take me
by the hand."

The first man to reach him was Henry Knox, the huge chief of
artillery, who silently held out his hand—but Washington im-
pulsively threw his arms about Knox and kissed him. He then
kissed all of the officers, from the German drillmaster Baron von
Steuben down to the youngest. During the wordless ceremony the
face of each man streamed with tears.

Washington left the embrace of the last of his officers, raised his
arm in farewell, and left the tavern. Outside he passed between
the ranks of a guard of honor. Then he passed down a street
packed on either side with thousands of men and women, many
of whom held up small children to look at the stern-faced general.
Washington stepped into a barge which was to take him across the
river to begin the trip southward to Mount Vernon. As it shoved
off he raised his arm once more in silent farewell. The crowd
could hear from across the harbor the squealing of boatswains'
whistles as the last of the British transports piped all hands aboard
and began to make sail for the voyage home.

The American people would not leave Washington in retirement. He was called to take a leading part in forming the federal
government, which he favored so strongly. In 1787 he became
chairman of the Constitutional Convention and did much to as-
sure the adoption of the new U.S. Constitution.

Two years later, by unanimous vote of the electors from the

thirteen original states, Washington was elected President. He handled the country's affairs with the same patient wisdom and sound judgment he had shown during the terrible years of the Revolution. He served eight years in the national capital of the day, New York City, but refused a third term and retired to Mount Vernon.

One December day in 1799 as Washington rode about his estate in a sleet storm he caught a severe cold. He soon went to bed, weak and feverish, with a sore throat and an ailment his doctor called "inflammatory quinsy." The general was bled several times in an effort to save his life, but the treatment seemed only to weaken him.

He died on December 14, just two weeks before the opening of the nineteenth century, in which the country to which he had devoted his life was to grow great. He was buried in the family vault at Mount Vernon overlooking the Potomac, the home from which he had gone off to war so long before.

Of all the heroes of the American Revolution, George Washington was the greatest. His iron will, his refusal to give up the cause however hopeless it seemed, his patience, dignity, and unselfish devotion won the respect of most Americans of his day. He was the one leader of the struggle for independence who seemed to be irreplaceable.

George Washington had a special gift for making the best of the talents of other men, and for bringing together those of different ideas and persuasions. Though his country was deeply divided, his influence was enough to win the public support needed for final victory. The young United States was fortunate to find in its crisis so capable and faithful a leader. Without him, the Revolution probably could not have been won.

As his cavalryman "Light-Horse" Harry Lee said after Washington's death, the Commander in Chief was "first in war, first in peace and first in the hearts of his countrymen."

Index ★ ★ ★ ★ ★

The pictures in this book were provided through the courtesy of: American Antiquarian Society, 28–29; American Philosophical Society, 37; Chicago Historical Society, 70–71; Colonial Williamsburg, 14–15, 67; Dietrich Foundation, 116–117; Dixon Ticonderoga Pencil Collection, 33; Historical Society of Pennsylvania, 38–39; Thomas Jefferson Memorial Foundation, Inc., 44; Nina Leen, *Life* Magazine © Time Inc., 42; Lexington Historical Society, 8–9; Library of Congress, front endpaper, facing false title, 47, 52–53, 138–139, 141; Mr. and Mrs. B. K. Little, 57; Metropolitan Museum of Art, gift of Collis P. Huntington, 131; Metropolitan Museum of Art, gift of William H. Huntington, 21, 68, 86; Metropolitan Museum of Art, bequest of Charles Allen Munn, false title, 27, 82, 85, 110; New York Historical Society, 97, 103, 135; New York Public Library, Emmet Collection, 58; New York Public Library, Print Room, 4–5, 12, 24, 61; New York State Historical Association, Cooperstown, copyright page, 80; Lawrence D. Thornton (from Frederick Lewis Agency), 136; United States Naval Museum, 104–105.

The maps on pages 90 and 119 are from *The History of the American Revolution* by John R. Alden. Copyright © 1969 by John R. Alden. Reprinted by permission of Alfred A. Knopf, Inc.

The cover photograph is by Dick Hanley (Photo Researchers).

Back endpaper: "Capture of the

About the Author ★ ★ ★ ★

Burke Davis is the author of many books on military subjects, including *Get Yamamoto, The Billy Mitchell Affair,* and *The Campaign That Won America: The Story of Yorktown.* His books for younger readers include *America's First Army* and *Thomas Jefferson's Virginia.*

"For many years," he says, "I have studied the Southern campaigns of the American Revolution, and I am familiar with most of the incidents and the battlefields. My ancestors in North Carolina fought on both sides of the conflict, and it has always held my interest."

Born in Durham, North Carolina, Mr. Davis studied at Duke University and at the University of North Carolina. He worked as a reporter, sports editor, and editor for newspapers in his native state and in Maryland. Since 1960 he has been on the staff of Colonial Williamsburg in Virginia.

Hessians at Trenton" by John Trumbull (Yale University Art Gallery).